Rose Marie Reid

AN EXTRAORDINARY LIFE STORY

Rose Marie Reid

AN EXTRAORDINARY LIFE STORY

by

Carole Reid Burr
and
Roger K. Petersen

Covenant Communications, Inc.

Published by Covenant Communications, Inc.
American Fork, Utah

Printed in the United States of America
First Printing: March 1995

01 00 99 98 97 96 95 94   10 9 8 7 6 5 4 3 2 1

ISBN 1-55503-810-7

DEDICATION

This book is gratefully dedicated to Rose Marie's sister, Marion Heilner, who provided the inspiration and love necessary to complete it. Her love for Rose Marie knew no bounds.

ACKNOWLEDGMENTS

We wish to express appreciation to the numerous people who took hours and sometimes days to be interviewed, who recreated their relationship with Rose Marie Reid in order that this work would be accurate and lasting.

To those who contributed many long hours of transcribing: Susan, Rose Marie, Lara, Sharon, and Joelle, five of Rose Marie Reid's granddaughters. They came to know and love her one page at a time.

To those who assisted in the research, read the manuscript, and offered their comments—especially Jan Warner, Ethan Barborka, JennaVee Crookston Gee, Dan Hogan, Richard Cracroft, Rose Marie Smith, and Max Thomas. Thank you.

To our spouses, Susan Petersen and James Burr, for their patience, and to our combined number of sixteen children who wondered at times if they would ever get their turn on the computer.

And to Valerie Holladay, a new friend and great editor who refined the manuscript with her own expertise. With innate sensitivity, Valerie recognized the extraordinary life story of Rose Marie Reid.

To all, we express our gratitude and love.

CONTENTS

Rose Marie Reid

FOREWORD

"Rose Marie Reid." The name was, and is, a marketplace name through the world. It is also a household word. And in a deeper sense, for that is where her heart was. I can demonstrate this with one memorable glimpse.

While on a Church history bus tour, we found ourselves in Independence, Missouri; the group asked if we could visit the Harry S. Truman Library. It was not on the agenda, but after a hasty phone call we were welcomed in.

The former president of the United States himself was there, and he led us to a small amphitheater. After a brief introduction or two (he may have recognized Rose Marie's name), President Truman stood at a lectern and said, "Let this be like a press conference. Fire away!"

We looked at each other wondering who would break the silence.

"Mr. President," Rose Marie began with a smile, "we are all Mormons"—he nodded recognition, and she continued, "—we think all good people should be Mormons. We wonder if anyone has ever—?"

"Yes," he interrupted, "and I think all good people should be Baptists. Next question!"

Someone asked about dropping the atomic bomb, and he justified it in one sentence. Another asked about the burdens of the Presidency. He responded that they were terribly heavy. Then Rose Marie spoke again, "Did you know that the Mormons believe they will be called again to settle here?"

"Yes," said the former president. "I've talked to your church president, and he has given me permission to stay!"

Rose Marie had one final question. "Mr. President, what do you know about the Mormons?"

He replied quickly, "I know they are honest and pay their debts."

In this one incident there is much of Rose Marie's personality. She was one of the most energetic and stay-with-it persons I have ever known. She could not be intimidated. Her preoccupation with her faith and her relentlessly patient efforts to live it—and just as much to share it—impressed even those who had little regard for religion. She was also drawn deeply into history and family history. Who else would build a home with a central space as her "genealogy room"? Her faith was her life. Phenomenal business success and reputation were sidelights. Her religion made her children her intimate and ultimate concern.

But Rose Marie could not define her family as one generation alone. On the scale of Alex Haley, she tried to uncover and honor her roots. She stretched her heart toward her forbears as well as her posterity. Whatever one could say about others who sat there that day, President Truman's reply to her was true of her. In her life and in her profession, she was honest. And, with rare sensitivity, to generations before and after her, she paid her debts.

Truman G. Madsen

PREFACE

I had such a pretty dream, Mother,
Such pretty and beautiful things:
Of a dear little nest in the meadow of rest
Where the birdie her lullaby sings. . . .

I saw there a beautiful angel,
All dressed in a silvery, white gown.
She touched me and spoke,
I quickly awoke. . . .

When I was a little girl, my mother always sang a lullaby that
has had special significance to me. In the lullaby, a child had a beautiful dream of an angel, and when the angel "touched her and
spoke, [she] quickly awoke," and found that the angel was her
mother.

In my childhood, I believed with all my heart that this lullaby
had been written uniquely about me and my mother. Even now, I
never sing the lullaby or even think of my mother in life or in
death, without visualizing her as that angel. An angel is someone
soft, lovely, and on a divine assignment. An angel testifies of lofty
things and brings more beauty to the world, literally or symboli-
cally. Simply stated, that was my mother—Rose Marie Reid.

Immediately following her death, I began receiving requests from
libraries and universities who wanted to be considered as the recipient of her memorabilia and life story. They felt that she would be a
valued addition to their new focus on the history and accomplish-

ments of women. Many were even creating new departments, in the realization that the time and need had come for this new emphasis.

Her wonderful designs, I knew, were a matter of record. I was aware, too, of the hundreds of articles and pictures available, but they sadly reflected only a small part of this versatile and many-faceted woman. Nowhere could anyone find complete and accurate information about Rose Marie Reid that could even begin to portray her with the dignity she deserved.

During this time I also received numerous letters, which shared not only sympathy but many accounts of people's experiences with her, wherein they described her love, her compassion, and her great gifts.

I was aware that, tragically, my mother had resisted telling her own story through a personal journal or diary. "There wasn't enough time," she would say, or "I can't re-live the experiences— some were simply too painful." She had wanted the positive and happy memories of her life to eclipse the negative memories, and she refused to engage in any renderings of her life story.

An instructor and historian at Brigham Young University made an attempt to interview her in order to preserve an oral history. Only a few months before the publication of this biography, he told me that in his classes he still uses her, fifteen years later, as an example of one of the most difficult interviews he ever conducted. She had learned the fine art of evading questions she did not want to answer.

Although it was difficult to interview her and he knew her oral history was neither complete nor accurate, this historian recognized that hers was a story that needed to be told. She had lived during a time when many of the challenges she had experienced, such as divorce and abuse, were not discussed. Divorce was not considered "respectable," and abuse was never acknowledged.

After he had completed Mother's oral history, he encouraged me to write her life story; and as the requests for it persisted and intensified, I began looking over all of her files. There were dozens of interviews, corporate minutes, newspaper and magazine articles, design layouts, court records, and personal correspondence (thank goodness the telephone had not entirely replaced the written word!). Looking over this vast array of information, I was keenly aware of my own inadequacies when it came to undertaking such a task. With nine children and many church and community obligations, I found it easy to make excuses to postpone this project. How, I wondered, could I sift through the information and relate it honestly and accurately with only a forgivable bias?

One of my answers and vital tools came through my work on a curriculum committee in The Church of Jesus Christ of Latter-day Saints. The chair of the committee, Roger K. Petersen, and I began to work together on this biography to gather the information into a whole. We met each week to share our writing and perspective. As he pored over the information, he soon caught the vision and spirit of this remarkable woman. I felt an understanding and a oneness of purpose with him, and we worked so well together that we could almost finish each other's sentences. He told me, "I wrote the facts and you made them sing."

Soon we both, in a harmonious way, felt her approval of what we were doing and how we were presenting her life. It was good to delve into the painful parts of her life, for the world is full of pain. It was appropriate to relate the moments of doubt, for in her experience those who doubt could find hope. And it was not misplaced to testify of God, even in the marketplace, for many are searching and need the witness that a Rose Marie Reid could give.

My mother's talents were endless, but her greatest gift was that she valued people the most. She treasured her association with people from all walks of life. Much of her life was humble and poor, and a good deal of it was extraordinarily successful. But through it all, she never lost sight of the infinite worth of every soul.

Of all the gifts she bequeathed to me personally, the greatest is an absolute assurance of my intrinsic personal worth. She did not speak of "self-esteem," or feel the need to teach it to others; "self-esteem," she felt, caused people to measure themselves against the successes and failures of others. She taught all those she knew that they had intrinsic self-worth: the inherent worth that comes from who we are. We are equal in the sight of God and have great value to one another. No one can take that away from us. This she helped me to understand, and I will love her eternally for that perfect gift.

We have written this biography of my mother so that all may share in the gift of her life.

Carole Reid Burr

CHAPTER 1

Elvie and Marie

Rose Marie Reid's link to her pioneer past is an interesting paradox because the name Rose Marie Reid was to become a symbol of the modern future. Yet, as modern as she grew to be, she remained deeply attached to her heritage and the legacy her ancestors left.

Throughout her life, Rose Marie was proud that she was a sixth-generation Mormon. Her great-grandmother, Maria Hadlond, left England in the 1840s to join members of The Church of Jesus Christ of Latter-day Saints in America, willingly leaving her homeland to help establish a new frontier in behalf of her newfound faith. Maria married Preston Thomas, eventually bearing him ten children.

Rose Marie's own great-grandfather, William Hyde, had personally known Joseph Smith (the founder of The Church of Jesus Christ of Latter-Day Saints, or Mormons, as they are frequently known). William Hyde had joined the Church in 1834 when he was just sixteen. When the Mormon Saints were being driven from Nauvoo, Illinois, he accompanied them on foot and eventually joined the Mormon Battalion. Making his way overland across the great Southwest, he reached California with the Battalion in late 1846. Following his return, he journeyed with his family to the Salt Lake Valley in the Utah Territory. There they joined with other Mormons who had left everything they possessed and sacrificed their former lives to find a location where they could be free to worship God without persecution.

Don Carlos Hyde, Rose Marie's grandfather, was sent by Brigham Young, Joseph Smith's successor, to settle in Cache Valley, Utah, where Don Carlos established Hyde Park.[1]

In 1890, Brigham Young requested that several members leave the Church's refuge in the Salt Lake valley and journey to Canada to establish a settlement that would extend the Church beyond the borders of the United States. Rose Marie's mother, Marie Hyde, was seven years old when she accompanied her family to Cardston, Alberta, walking behind a covered wagon.

The meeting and marriage of Rose Marie's parents is a true love story. Her father, William Elvie Yancey, came to Cardston by accident. He had followed his family to Salt Lake from Mississippi, where his parents, Jasper and Sarah Francis Tunnel Yancey, had heard the gospel message from a young Mormon missionary, George Albert Smith, who later became prophet and president of the Mormon Church.

Smith enountered a great deal of bitterness against the Mormons in Mississippi, and the Yancey family was one of only two families in the state who let the missionaries sleep in their home. In fact, they often kept a pile of blankets in a corner of their living room, and as the missionaries slept, Jasper and his brother sat by the door with shotguns on their laps to protect the missionaries from the angry mobs who often persecuted Church members.

After the Yanceys were at last baptized, they sold their farm in Mississippi and traveled west to Salt Lake to join with the other Church members. However, William Elvie was not baptized, and he did not approve of his parents' membership in the Church. Resentful of his parents' decision to embrace a new and unpopular religion, he set out to disprove the doctrine. Instead, he was ultimately baptized into the Mormon faith.

William Elvie followed his parents to Salt Lake, then decided to return to Mississippi when he met the family of Hugh B. Brown (Brown later became an Apostle of the Church). The Brown family was preparing to travel by wagon to Canada and somehow persuaded Elvie to join the trek. As they traveled they taught him the restored gospel, and by the time he met Marie he had gained a testimony of the Prophet Joseph Smith and the restoration of the church of Jesus Christ. After he was baptized, he decided to remain with the members in Cardston and help to establish the Church there.

Marie first met Elvie when her Sunday School class was out for a sleigh ride. When the reins somehow slipped from the driver's hands, young Elvie—tall, straight, and nearly twenty-eight years old with handsome dark reddish hair—gathered in the reins from the sleigh's edge and handed them back to the driver. Marie, only seventeen, looked out from under the blankets in the sleigh and told her friends, "That's the man I'm going to marry."[2]

Elvie shared Marie's impression. As their courtship progressed, he penned a letter to her from the Clarke Coal Mines on 6 December 1899. "While I am working in those dark halls," he wrote, "my mind reflects upon our earliest acquaintance, of how. . . the fires of love were first kindled in my bosom." Elvie's letters, all inscribed in his beautiful penmanship, bespeak a man of deep and worthy intent. He continued: "My whole being seemed to be inspired with new thought, in fact I seemed to be filled with new life, I became a new being. At this time my heart was filled with exceeding joy and gladness. You were vividly pictured in my mind, and something seemed to speak very loudly in my ear and said 'Elvie Yancey you are certainly a fortunate person to meet your bosom companion.'"[3]

The winter was filled with sweet meetings between the young couple, who met at the bridge, on the pond, and sometimes at home with Marie's parents. By spring, they were ready to marry. Don Carlos, Marie's father, announced the marriage for Thursday, 29 March 1900. The newspaper reported a lovely wedding, complete with "Wagnerian music" and the Wolseys, a local family, singing a lilting tune to "guitar accompaniment" in their "usual pleasing style." The couple reportedly started their marriage "as in a bower of roses."[4] Their only regret was the absence of a temple sealing, so coveted by young Mormon couples to ensure their marriage for time and on into eternity.

After their marriage, Elvie continued working in the mines. To save money, letters were often hand-delivered by friends and neighbors going back and forth to town. To deliver a letter for Marie, her father once entered the Black Diamond mine, where he was struck by the blackness of the mine. Elvie, however, could make $5.50 a day, which was enough to pay the bills and prepare for their first baby.

The letters between them are revealing. Marie, for example, was fairly self-conscious. Though she was always regarded as a beautiful woman, she felt that she was plain of face. Elvie's response to her concerns was, "I never cared much for fashion plated or drugstore complexions. I believe that Marie looks well enough for me."[5] Throughout their separation, Elvie deeply missed Marie. "I dream of my Darling almost every night. . . ."[6]

Knowing that Marie was expecting their first child, he wrote: "I know that should you get hurt now you would never be strong and healthy again, but perhaps an invalid as long as you may live. You can't be too careful any how." His concerns were not only for her health, but for the child as well: "Cultivate in yourself whatsoever you desire to see in your offspring; for the thoughts, actions, desires, and appetites of the mother is inherited by her children. Be very careful that you never get melancholy or vexed, take plenty of exercise, practice music, read good wholesome literature or something that is ennobling and elevating to the mind, for one's posterity is influenced by every thought of its mother." Elvie often waxed eloquent, as in the following: "'When should a child's education begin?' The philosopher's answer, 'Two thousand years before the child is born.'"[7]

That their love was growing and maturing can be seen in Elvie's words just before Christmas. "When I wrote you the little poem 'Love is like a tree' I, at that time, thought that I did really know what love is. But I had no conception of it then as compared with the present time."[8]

Separation was so hard for the young couple that it was not long before Elvie decided to leave the mines and homestead a dry farm. The home on the farm was little more than a shanty, and the country was so vast and sparsely settled that people leaving from Elvie's land could travel two thousand miles without seeing a fence. The plains looked like an ocean of waving grass. Elvie Jr. recalled a time when he looked out at his father's lake and thought it had dried up because it appeared so black. As he ran to see what had happened,

Marie Yancey and daughter Rose Marie

the whole surface of the lake began to move, then exploded into a black sky of flying ducks and geese.

The winters were extremely cold, and came so quickly with their violent hailstorms that often the beautiful wheat crops were entirely wiped out when not yet ripe enough to harvest. At the same time, the growing season was so short that it was impossible to grow a variety of vegetables or fruits.

After giving birth to three sons, Marie at last presented Elvie Sr. with a baby daughter on 12 September 1906. They named her Rose Marie Yancey. Elvie Jr., a young boy of four at her birth, would remember for many years "how beautiful [Rose] was sweetly lying in Mamma's arms; how proud Papa was, after having three sons, to have a lovely daughter."[9]

Life was hard for the young family. Elvie Jr. recalled that "[having] very little income, [Father] tried to make some money on the

Rose Marie and Marion Yancey

side doing carpenter work. One time Father went off doing carpentry, and Mother insisted on doing the harrowing. I remember Mother hitched up the horses, and she was seven months pregnant. One of the horses got frightened and started to run away. She got tangled in the lines, and was dragged for some distance. She started having labor pains, and Father came home and took her to Cardston. There Marion was born."

Marion, born three years after Rose Marie, was her dearest and closest friend. The two sisters loved each other enormously. "She would help me and care for me. She was a great teacher," said Marion. "I loved her dearly . . . because she made everything seem right for me. She was so bright. She helped me with my studies, but mostly she'd tell me I was beautiful, that I was smart, that my hair was the prettiest. I knew all along that she was the beautiful one, but she made me feel that I was. And I think she really thought it was true. . . ."[10]

Even later in life, it was painful for the two to be apart. Rose Marie often wrote Marion from New York and other distant locations, pleading, "Please come for Thanksgiving" or for Christmas, or what ever the occasion was.[11]

Growing up, the two girls slept together in the same bed every night until the day Rose Marie was married, and Rose Marie often read Marion stories. Said Marion, "We would always fold ourselves together, and I would snuggle into that sweet, nice, warm sister. She would put her arm around me. She acted like that was the loveliest privilege in the world."

As a girl, Rose Marie loved to read. "She read nearly every book in Cardston," said Marion. Since electricity was so expensive, lights were only allowed on at certain times, and the family rule allowed no electricity on in the bedrooms. But Rose would quietly turn on the light so she could read, shading the light with the blanket so Marion would not be disturbed.

Throughout her childhood, Rose was given tasks sometimes beyond her years. When she herself was not even four years old, she was caring for her brothers and sisters, both older and younger than herself. Said Elvie Jr., "We knew we were to take care of her, but it wasn't long before she was taking care of us."

On one occasion, Rose and Marion went sleigh riding with a neighborhood friend. The older girls were so busy talking that they didn't see little Marion start down a steep hill. As Marion gained momentum, she grew frightened, and a stray dog who chased after her down the hill scared her even worse.

As Marion screamed in terror, Rose raced after her, but she couldn't catch the sleigh until Marion at last came to an abrupt and painful halt by running into a barbed-wire fence. The barbs went through her clothes, and she carried the scars throughout her life.

Rose Marie was brokenhearted as she took Marion back to their mother. She felt that somehow it was all her fault, and that she had failed in her responsibility to care for her sister.

Rose also took Marion to school on her first day. Marion, however, was so frightened that she ran home at recess and made up a story about the boys tripping her. When Rose Marie came home at noon, Marie told her to go back to school and tell the teacher what the boys had done to Marion.

"I was scared to death that she was going to tell the teacher and I'd get whipped for lying," said Marion. But Rose Marie understood Marion's fear and simply stayed by her side at school. Rose Marie's protective instincts for Marion, and for others, continued throughout both of their lives.

As she grew older, Rose Marie hurried to complete her school studies early in the year so she could spend most of her time helping her mother and father make a living for the family. She always knew her support was sorely needed. It never occurred to Rose that she worked harder and longer than most other children. She matured quickly, and in spite of her naturally buoyant nature, she grew up with a reserved side to her personality. At times, she was deeply contemplative.

From a very early age, Rose Marie learned to be prayerful about her world. One year on the fourth of July, the family could see a violent hailstorm advancing across the valley. The children were frightened, for they could see the storm approaching. Elvie was away doing carpentry work, so Marie gathered the children together. They knelt in prayer and asked that the storm be stayed. Together they watched as the storm approached. It came right to their fence, then turned and passed exactly along the fence line, never touching their crops. These early experiences influenced Rose Marie so deeply that she always depended on prayer to direct her life. Through the years she came to understand and completely trust in God.

Many favorite stories of Rose Marie's childhood were her experiences with prayer. She often told of the time she and her little friend got lost, and the two knelt down beside their doll buggies. They told Father in Heaven that they were lost, and asked if he would please take them home. When they stood up, they knew exactly where to go. Another time, Rose Marie felt something terrible was going to happen to her family. She climbed out of her bed and told Heavenly Father "that He must not let it happen!" She later learned that her mother had been on the verge of total collapse because of her heavy workload. Rose's prayers had strengthened her mother, helping to avert a tragedy. Rose always told about the time the family needed money so badly that she prayed and prayed they would be able to sell their horse. The horse had a terrible temperament, but it was all they had to sell. A man came and offered them $100 for the horse, bad temperament and all. The amount was exactly what the family needed.

Her grandparents recognized Rose's goodness even at this early age. Grandma Hyde always told Marie that she must prepare for

Rose to die young, because a child that good could not be expected to live. Marie actually believed for quite some time that her daughter would die. Years later during an interview, Rose Marie laughed and said, "I guess I got bad enough to live."[12]

Marriage for eternity is greatly desired by faithful Mormons, and is considered such a sacred ordinance that it is only performed in a temple of God. For years it was something that Marie and Elvie had longed for. In 1908, they were finally able to take their four small children—Elvie Jr., Oliver, Hugh, and little Rose Marie—and return to Salt Lake City for this important sealing ordinance. This time, instead of riding in covered wagons, Marie rode on the train with her family. Rose Marie was only a toddler at the time, and the family in Utah was charmed by her, calling her the most beautiful child they had ever seen. Elvie Jr. was deeply touched by the beautiful temple and the sealing ceremony where the family was dressed in beautiful white clothing. He recalled meeting new relatives and was impressed with the pears and apples he could pick off the trees in Utah, something he had never before seen.

Another sacred ordinance for Mormons is baptism. According to Mormon doctrine, children cannot be held accountable for their choices until the age of eight, so baptism in the Mormon Church is never performed prior to that time. Children preparing for baptism are taught the sacredness of the experience so that they will always remember and cherish the promises and covenants made during the baptism ordinance. Young Marion remembers when she walked with her family down to Lee's Creek, just outside of Cardston, to witness Rose Marie's baptism. Marion held Rose Marie's little umbrella that had been given to her as a gift, and Rose Marie went under the water and came up looking as beautiful as she had before going under. Years later, Marion could still remember the umbrella and "how beautiful Rose looked."

Rose Marie's years in Cardston were filled with good experiences. The summers were rich with the beauties of wild geese, mountain grouse, deer and elk, and the fields were full of waving grass and a hundred varieties of flowers. Rose Marie would often go out into the wild flowers and sit for hours to think. The family was happy although they were poor, fruit and vegetables were scarce, and the winters were unbelievably cold and long. But it was here that Elvie and Marie began their family; here they nurtured and loved each other. In the future finances would improve, but there was never a happier time for Rose Marie. Later, she would intentionally block out some painful parts of her life, even when interviewed by historians. But she always loved to tell about Cardston, because it was a happy memory.

Notes

1. Family History of William Hyde, n.p., n.d., p. 45.
2. Marie Yancey, Personal History, n.d.
3. William Elvie Yancey, letter to Marie Hyde. William's letters to Marie are dated 22 October 1899 through 9 January 1900 (Clark Coal Mine). Hereafter referred to as Yancey Letters.
4. *Cardston News*, 30 March 1900. (Rose Marie frequently collected news clippings, but she did not not always note dates or page numbers.)
5. Yancey letters.
6. Ibid.
7. Ibid.
8. Ibid.
9. William Elvie Yancey, Jr., typed manuscript from interviews with the authors, 29 August 1988. All subsequent comments from William Elvie Yancey are taken from this source.
10. Marion Yancey Heilner, typed manuscript from interviews with the authors, 13 February 1988. All subsequent comments from Marion Heilner are taken from this source unless otherwise noted.
11. Rose Marie Reid to Marion Heilner, letter dated 13 February 1954 (New York City).
12. Rose Marie Reid, Oral History, p. 24.

Marie (pregnant with Rose Marie) and Elvie Sr., with three sons (left to right): Elvie Jr., Hugh, and Oliver. Marie designed and sewed all of the clothes for her young family and herself.

CHAPTER 2

Family Gifts

Whenever Rose Marie was interviewed, the questions most frequently asked were about her education, her training, and the development of her designing skills. She always answered that her schooling came from living life itself, her talent came from her mother, her eloquence she attributed to her father, and her courage and inspiration came from God. It may not have been the anticipated response or the answer that many would understand, but in fact, it was the truth.

Rose Marie's mother was the first in the family to design and sew for a living. Marie taught herself to sew through a correspondence course. When the people in the community wanted something original or particularly beautiful, they called upon Marie—even though almost everyone in the community sewed for themselves. Marie never used a pattern; she could simply visualize what needed to be done. She would just cut out what was wanted from the fabric given her and charge customers only for her time.

Her daughter Marion said, "To watch Mother was a real experience. Her customers would send her their beautiful fabrics from all over the province, and she would tell them she did not want a pattern; they needed only to send their measurements. She would spread the expensive material out on a table and tell all the children to be very quiet so she could think in her mind exactly how to cut the fabric. Then she would cut so quickly, like lightening, exactly as she had visualized it to be. It always ended up to be beautiful."

It seemed to Rose Marie that her mother was always sewing: "At first she would sew and I tended the children," Rose Marie later wrote. "Then I began to sew beside her. If she had lived at my time, she would have been a much better designer than I was."[1]

The family could not afford to buy new fabrics, but they always had leftover pieces of material. Beneath Marie's skillful hands, these became beautiful creations. Marion recalled that she and her brothers and sisters were always dressed beautifully. In addition to skirts, blouses, pinafores, and trousers, Marie even made little umbrellas. Although there came a time when Rose Marie had to make clothes for her own children out of flour sacks, the children were nevertheless always beautifully dressed. Years later, Rose Marie's children would arrive at their Brentwood mansion in Los Angeles, wearing underpants made from flour sacks.[2]

Rose Marie loved working beside her mother. Anything else she would "hurry up" to finish so that they could sew together.

Marie entertained her children by giving them scraps of material. They made doll clothes, and Marie saw to it that they did the designing themselves, with just a little advice from her. While they sewed, Marie told them stories and played dolls with them. The dolls were named Mrs. Brown and Mrs. Black. They went to social teas, to the theater, and, of course, to church, all while playing at their mother's feet. When Marie got tired, the boys would work the treadle of the sewing machine. "Mrs. Green is tired now," Marie would say. "Do you suppose Mr. Elvie could work the treadle for her for a while?"

The children took great delight in this world of make-believe. Sometimes they would go up to the old trunk in the attic and take out the spray of mock orange blossoms Marie had carried at her wedding. The children would march up and down the aisle of the attic in a bridal train made from scraps of curtain.

Sewing was also a time of schooling. When one child tired from sewing, he or she traded places and read to the other. The children read from the Book of Mormon, the Bible, and the classics. They read poetry and prose and textbooks. So enlightening was this for Rose Marie that years later she continued this habit. While design-

Family home in Weiser, Idaho

ing, she taught and instructed her models as they worked, and they all read to each other.

Whatever Marie did, Rose Marie was always beside her. When Rose was just ten and the family had moved to Idaho from Canada, the pair became so efficient at packing fruit for a local distributor that they were sought out especially for their speed and skill. The farmers in the area contended that the two of them could replace four others. Rose Marie stood on an apple crate so she could reach the apples and pack the bottom layer of the box. "Mother then topped the box," said Marion. All the money earned went to the family.

Marie had a garden that fed the family. In addition to caring for the garden, one year when Elvie couldn't get the harvesters to gather in a barley crop, Marie said to the girls, "We are going out to cut that barley."

Marie would do any chore necessary to keep the farm running, from ploughing and planting to caring for the animals. Many times Marie and her children, alone on the dry farm, could hear coyotes and even see them standing on the rim of the hill. But she never let the children know she was afraid.

Marie's family home was always spotless. She had an uncanny ability to fix or remodel nearly anything. She reinforced furniture

Marion and Rose Marie with the family car.
In the Yancey family, only the women drove.

and hovered over her husband until he fixed what she couldn't. Sometimes the ceilings had only cheesecloth separating the family from the rafters, but every inch of the rafters was whitewashed.

Marie insisted that the children be well mannered and speak with proper grammar. They had to be clean in appearance. Marie often sent little Rose Marie on errands, and she insisted that her daughter look beautiful before she left. Rose had curly golden hair, and Marie always kept it combed beautifully. Even when Rose had to walk the nine miles along the dusty road to town, she carried her little black shoes and then put them on so she would look neat and tidy when she arrived. One time she walked to town to deliver some butter to a friend. She remembered walking all the way in her pretty little dress and neatly combed hair, licking the butter.

Family outings were enjoyable experiences. Marie always did the driving. The whole family often loaded into the car—first an old Hudson, later an Essex, then a Ford—and drove 72 miles to Boise to eat at Macanifay's, a New York-style restaurant. They usually had two or three flat tires on the way, but it was worth it because the whole family could eat all they wanted for sixty cents.

At night, the family sat in the kitchen around the table while Elvie helped the children practice their penmanship and read the scriptures to them. Marie helped them prepare little talks for church or they all sang together. The girls reached the point where they could sing duets and trios while Rose Marie accompanied them on the piano. Every morning at 5:30 a.m., the family would wake to Rose Marie practicing the piano. She became an accomplished pianist, and the family was surrounded by her wonderful music. She even played the piano for the local theatre. Newspapers of the era show that Joan Crawford's movie *Rose Marie* came to town during a time when Rose Marie was the theatre accompanist. Though we have no record of her feelings at this event, it must have been significant for her. How could Rose Marie even guess that one day she would design for Joan Crawford?

Rose Marie's sister Marion said of their childhood, "I think what I remember most is how Mama taught all of the children to revere their father and depend on Papa's priesthood. [The priesthood, for members of the Mormon faith, is the power to act in God's name, to perform Church ordinances, bless the sick, and carry out other duties of service.] How grateful she was for that priesthood in our home."

Following Elvie's conversion to the gospel, he had become an avid gospel scholar and scriptorian. Few had his mastery and eloquence for teaching the gospel. Rose Marie remembered that her father served not only as bishop of their ward (a Mormon congregation) but also taught in the Sunday School. "My father . . . was the best teacher of all. . . . I thought we already had the best teacher in the world, and then my father taught us and he was so much better than anyone else. I was so proud of him. I just looked at everybody else in the class and thought, 'Can't you just see how marvelous he is?'"[3]

Elvie always regretted not having the opportunity to serve a mission for his church. He taught his children to be very mindful of those who were not members. Not all of the family's neighbors were Mormons, and sometimes they ridiculed Church members. Elvie, however, never let the children speak ill of their non-Mormon neighbors. He taught his children to care for them. "Be kind and polite. They don't understand and are only seeking what you already have," said their father.[4]

Elvie taught all the children to have respect for the Church and its leaders. According to Marion, "We had to leave Weiser [Idaho] at about 4:00 in the morning [to get to Church conference].

Because the dust would get in the car, we would have to take our clothes with us that we would wear. . . .We would drive to the park and go to the restrooms and change our clothes. All the way our father would tell us who was going to be there, and if it was one of the Apostles we would be told what a special and sacred time it would be and how fortunate we were going to be to see an Apostle of the Lord. And we learned to love all of those men and respect them because of all of that teaching that Mother and Father would give us." Little Rose Marie could never have imagined that later many great Church apostles would actually be guests in her own home!

If Elvie had a fault, it was his trusting nature. Nor did he manage money well. In fact, he seemed not to care about it. He owned two grocery stores in his life, but he extended credit to everyone and in so doing gave away most of the inventory. His dry farms failed, and his chicken business, which he started later in Baker, Oregon, was a disaster. He was a good carpenter, a concerned neighbor, and a wonderful bishop. Elvie Jr. said of his father, "He was a friend of everyone, [he was] cheerful, he loved everybody, and tried to do good to everyone. . . . He was an inspiration."

While Elvie worked in the fields beside his children, he would quiz them hour after hour. They would play math games and have spelling contests. This paid great dividends at school and in life. Elvie Jr. became a champion speller, and Rose Marie was able to complete her schoolwork many times faster than her schoolmates. She developed the capacity for remembering details and figuring quickly—an ability that later served her well in the business world.

Elvie loved his wife deeply. He never passed her chair without reaching out and touching her, kissing her, or putting his arms around her. He was patriarchal and princely, and his children respected him. Elvie's life and legacy to his family was honesty, virtue, and integrity. He raised his family with his priesthood power, healing them when they were ill and teaching them of God.

One day, Marion remembered seeing her father approaching the house from the fields. It was too early for him to have completed his work, so Marie ran out to meet him. He said, "Mama, we need to go to the Olsen home, for their father has just passed on and the family will need us." Marie inquired how he knew of this death.

Elvie responded that the man's spirit had stopped to tell him farewell while Elvie was working in the fields, and he had requested that they take care of his loved ones.[5] Elvie and Marie quickly responded and found the man's family in need of comfort and other care. It seemed that spiritual experiences were common occurrences for this humble father as well as for the entire Yancey family.

From her parents, Rose Marie received a heritage of spirituality and creativity. Indeed, her entire lineage appears to have bequeathed her with rich gifts, as proclaimed in her patriarchal blessing. These blessings, given by patriarchs in the Mormon Church, reveal to the recipients their gifts and talents from God, directions to proceed so they might bless the earth's inhabitants, and the outcome of their obedience. Rose Marie was told in her blessing, "Your veins are filled with very rich blood. The gentleness of Abraham and Isaac, the acumen of Jacob and Judah, and the tenderness and the initiative of Joseph and Ephraim all mingle within thee, and thou art overflowing with all their gifts."[6]

Rose Marie's inherited gifts and talents were enhanced by the love and training of her parents. Her father instilled in her a love for all people and an ability to articulate her beliefs. Her refined and lovely mother was reflected in every creation Rose Marie made. With these gifts, the parents of Rose Marie Yancey Reid set their daughter on a path that would lead to international acclaim and personal religious devotion.

Notes

1. Rose Marie Reid, Oral History, p. 16.
2. Sharon Reid Alden, interview, n.d. All subsequent comments from Sharon Alden are from this source unless otherwise noted.
3. Rose Marie Reid, Oral History, p.16.
4. William Elvie Yancey, Jr., interview.
5. Marion Heilner, interview.
6. Rose Marie Reid, Patriarchial Blessing. Given by Charles H. Norberg, 7 June 1951.

Young Rose Marie (at age 15) was a beauty/talent show winner.

CHAPTER 3

A Driven, Young Businesswoman

In 1916, Elvie Sr. moved his family from Canada to Weiser, Idaho. There he purchased two pieces of property and homesteaded a third. The homestead was nine miles outside of Wieser and consisted of 160 acres of dry land. No matter how hard the family worked, the farm robbed them of precious and scarce resources. For ten years they toiled on the farm, and when they finally gave up the homestead, they all knew they had invested too much for too long. Rose Marie learned from these experiences in her young life. Many years later, she wrote in a letter to Ruth, her youngest sister, "There is one rule we learn in business and by experience. . . . If there is a loss to be taken, take it quickly, and go on to other operations that can be profitable."[1]

In response to her hard work, the family began to rely on her, and from an early age Rose Marie felt herself responsible for the temporal and spiritual welfare of her family. "I don't know if everyone expected it of her or if she just took it upon herself," said her daughter Carole. "But it was as if she felt that everyone's welfare was her divine assignment." It was an assignment that she took very seriously indeed. An assignment she would fulfil as long as she lived.

Rose Marie worked at everything so she could contribute to the family income. It never occurred to her to keep any of the money she earned for herself; she just naturally thought that anything she earned was "family money." When an epidemic of smallpox hit

Wieser, fifteen-year-old Rose Marie continued to work even though she herself was ill. She did not understand the danger of the disease, and the necessity of gaining income drove her. Even at the peak of her business career in future years, she would frequently observe, "It is not my money. It was not given to me for myself. It was to share and benefit the lives of everyone, especially the family."

Her father did have one financial success. After the loss of the dry farm, one piece of property he had purchased near Monroe Creek doubled in value, and he was able to sell the property for $4,000. With this money he bought the Midway Grocery. Marie established a small alteration and design shop in a front room, and the family's finances immediately began to improve. It was not long until Elvie sold the store and purchased the larger and better located Commercial Grocery on Main Street. Rose Marie was only fourteen when she helped manage the family stores.

One year later, she and her mother also opened a small beauty shop in their home. They named it "Rose Marie's," and Rose went away to Boise to learn beauty work. Marie found it hard to accept the fact that her fifteen-year-old daughter was living seventy-two miles away from home to improve a family business. But she knew no other way, as both mother and daughter were driven to support the family. The experience heightened Rose Marie's sense of responsibility. Having experienced poverty, she was afraid of it, and knew her family needed her desperately.

This early work experience also gave Rose Marie the opportunity to make several discoveries that she would use throughout her life to help others feel more beautiful. Because there were so many things about herself she didn't like (especially her freckles), she worked extra hard at her appearance and learned how to compensate for what she felt was her lack of natural beauty. Long before "ratting," or back-combing, became popular, Rose Marie learned that it gave body and thickness to her hair.

She was also afflicted with recurring eczema that was so painful she could only sleep after having received a comforting blessing from her father. When she was home, her mother would wrap her cracked hands and feet in grease.

Elvie Jr.'s decision to serve a mission for the Mormon Church meant an added financial burden for the family, as the support for the missionary was always provided by one's own family. Rose's family increased their efforts and their faith, for they all believed in the importance of this mission. To help in this effort, Rose Marie participated in a competition that was both a beauty and talent contest and a subscription drive for a local movie theater. The prize was one hundred silver dollars. Contestants were to solicit subscriptions to the theater, then appear for a beauty and talent show.

The competition was keen. Rose Marie's chief competitors were a pair of beautiful twin sisters who were working together to win the prize. Rose Marie, however, was determined not to lose; she worked until her feet were sore and cracked from walking. While she was less concerned with the beauty and talent aspects of the contest, she was afraid the other girls would outsell her.

It was, however, Rose Marie who finally won. She proudly brought home the bag of silver dollars, which was "nearly as big as she was," according to Elvie Jr. The family was jubilant! Not only did her prize assist Elvie on his mission, but it also paid for her mother's passage to Cardston to witness the dedication of the Mormon temple there. Marie was thrilled that this holy privilege had come to the town that she and her family had pioneered.

Keeping Elvie Jr. on his mission cost the family seventy-five dollars every month for two years. One month they simply couldn't earn the money. However, a near disaster turned into a blessing for them. One day, when Marion and her younger sister, Ruth, were sitting at home by the stove trying to stay warm, they suddenly heard a crackling noise and smelled smoke. Both girls ran out of the house and tried to call for help, although Marion found she had lost her voice completely.

The fire was in their mother's bedroom where the chimney flue went into the ceiling. Elvie had always feared a fire and insisted that the family keep buckets of water at all times throughout the house. Had it not been for these strategically placed buckets, it would have been necessary to go outside and prime the pump to get water. But Marion took one of those full buckets and threw it at the flame. She always said, "God threw that first bucket!" It was thrown in a way that subdued the flames until help could come. Seeing the smoke and hearing the alarm, Elvie Sr. ran a mile to get to the fire. Marie was frantic thinking of the loss, but was thankful that her children were safe. The family always regarded the fire as a miracle, however, for the insurance money was used for their missionary, and Elvie could do the repairs himself.

Financially, it was almost impossible for the children to go to college. The boys had a choice between missions and schooling, but the girls' role was to assist the family. Rose Marie's older brother Hugh was determined to study at the university, so in the fall of 1922 he enrolled at the University of Idaho in Moscow.

After several weeks the family realized they had heard nothing from Hugh. Marie was frantic. Somehow they learned that Hugh had left school and traveled to Aberdeen, Washington, to work in the lumber camps.

Said Marion, "Papa and Mama were so upset, for they had terrible fears of the influence in those camps; some of the roughest characters in the world worked there." Marie immediately took Rose Marie and Marion in the family Ford and started for Aberdeen. Little did they know they were driving into the famous Tellemut Forest fire. But nothing would stop Marie. Burning logs fell on either side of the road, threatening to hit the car. When Marie finally located Hugh, he was black from soot and sun, and painfully thin. Marie fell upon him and said "Hugh, you come home."

"I just couldn't do it," Hugh admitted to Marie.

"You don't have to. Just come home." And so Hugh returned with them and prepared instead for his mission.[2]

Hugh purchased for Rose Marie the only Christmas present—a beautiful gold pen—she ever recalled receiving as a child. Hugh was also the beloved father figure for Rose Marie's children as they grew up in Southern California.

Tragedy struck the family when Oliver, Rose Marie's brother just older than herself, became fatally ill. He was only sixteen years old and was much like Rose Marie in temperament and facial features. "Oliver was too perfect to live," Rose Marie always told her children. "He was a peacemaker and the most wonderful brother." He had been working in the melon fields, and one night he didn't return home. Elvie went looking for him and found him writhing in pain. His appendix had ruptured, shooting poison throughout his body. Oliver pleaded with his father to cut him open to remove the pain, but all Elvie could do was lay his hands on his son's head and dedicate him to the Lord. The day before Memorial Day 1918, Oliver uttered prophetically to his mother, "Tomorrow you will be putting flowers on my grave." He lingered, however, and died the day after Memorial Day.

Marie sewed his white burial clothes and Elvie built his coffin. Marie deeply mourned Oliver's death, but the family observed that she never shed a tear. She became quiet and stoic, sometimes even bitter. One year later, when her last child, Don, was born (a son following three girls), Marie softened and said, "The Lord has sent me a little boy to fill my empty arms and to take Oliver's place."[3]

The following years brought many changes for the family. They moved into a larger home on Main Street, and in September 1925 purchased the Della Esham's Millinery and Ready to Wear Store and Beauty Parlor, as reported by the Weiser newspaper. "Having bought the Della Esham Millinery and Ready to Wear Store and Beauty Parlor," the article stated, "business will continue with the addition of a hemstitching department."[4] The new business was named after the family, "Yanceys'."

As the new venture expanded, the beauty salon was moved to separate premises. Some even traveled long distances for the beauty services of the Yancey women. Later Marie learned of a popular salon for sale in Baker City, Oregon, and made the one-hour drive to investigate the possibility of purchasing the business to accommodate their long-distance customers. When she came back, she announced that they were now the proud owners of two salons. Rose Marie and Marion alternately traveled to Baker to work in their new business. Although Marion was young and frightened of staying there alone at night, Rose Marie was fearless—a conditioning for the many nights she would later spend alone in her downtown Los Angeles factory on Santee Street.

While the Yancey women were thus engaged, the Yancey brothers and a traveling "speed artist" named Garreth Rhynhart set up a painting studio in a side room of the Baker salon. With the family involved in so many endeavors, life looked promising.

Nevertheless, Rose Marie was conscious that her own success was giving her brothers an "inferiority complex." Her brothers, she felt, were "despondent" at the lack of success in finding good jobs, and she and her mother were "terrified" that her brothers would try to find work in a lumber camp "which seemed to be the only work open."[5]

The Yancey family had known Garreth Rhynhart in Canada, and Rose Marie's brothers "begged him to teach them to paint fast." At first Garreth refused to take any money, but then after two weeks he refused to give more lessons. Always "artistically inclined," the boys were "desperately anxious to finish." When Rose Marie asked Garreth why he would not give them any more lessons, he claimed that he was in love with her and had only agreed to teach them to be near her. She responded, "My obligation to my family [is] so great I couldn't marry anyone for years." But when he said that he wouldn't teach her brothers anymore, and that the boys "could not go on the road and make any money with the limited training they now had," she relented, after three days of tearful and hard thinking.[6]

Since Garreth already had a steady income with his beautiful landscape painting business, Elvie and Marie saw Garreth as a good Mormon boy who had the ability to make a good living for their daughter. Elvie Sr. himself arranged for the wedding license bureau to open on Sunday, and as Rose Marie's bishop, he performed the wedding—all within a few hours of their decision to marry.

Elvie Jr. was not at home when the marriage took place. When he returned, he was furious. He saw her marriage to Garreth as an act of personal sacrifice on Rose Marie's part, as Garreth now agreed to continue to teach her brothers to paint. Rose Marie later wrote of the experience: "When my brothers learned of the marriage, they were so furious; and it took days of persuasion on my part to convince them that I was not sorry (for their artistic training made them a good living all during the Depression)." Because Garreth continued to teach her brothers, "they were able to set themselves up in other businesses and are happily married, with fine families."[7] Because of their training, both brothers were able to survive the Depression, and both painted professionally the remainder of their lives. (Hugh and his wife, Elinor, died in 1966 on a military transport plane off the coast of Alaska, where he was entertaining the U.S. troops with his paintings.)

Only later did the Yancey family learn that Garreth had threatened to stop teaching Rose Marie's brothers and leave the area unless she married him.

True to her religious beliefs concerning the importance of temple marriage, Rose Marie married Garreth in the Salt Lake City temple a short while after their civil marriage. As she went through the temple with Garreth, she kept saying to herself, "Just one more room—I'll love him in the next room." But she found that she could not.

The three Yancey daughters all encountered sorrows in their marriages. Marion married a good man, but he was nonetheless not of the Mormon faith, and she mourned it all of her life. Ruth, the youngest daughter, married three times searching for happiness. Ironically, these marriages were probably troubled in part because of their father, Elvie Sr., whose example as a husband to Marie was hard to follow. These young girls must have felt only disillusionment when comparing their husbands to him. Elvie Sr. had been the perfect husband and father, but the men his daughters married were not, nor were many of the other men who came into Rose Marie's life.

The late 1920s and early 30s brought financial disaster for the Yancey family. The local bank collapsed, and the family's savings were lost. Marie felt the loss perhaps more deeply than anyone, as it represented years of her family's hard work and sacrifice. The family began to break up and move to other areas. Elvie tried to financially secure his family through an ill-fated venture into chicken farming in Baker City. Garreth and Rose Marie also started chicken farming in Salem, Oregon, on a farm that had been owned by a former governor of Oregon named McNary. Rose Marie's memory of this experience was bitter. They were forced to eat chicken feed to survive, and the businesses failed miserably because of the Depression.

Next, the Yancey family heard that a naturally occurring crystal formation, which could easily be made into an elixir, had been discovered in Texas. The crystals, called Krazy Krystals, became quite popular as a health tonic and medicinal aid, and soon the whole family became involved in marketing the elixir. Even Hugh, who had returned from his mission, assisted. Elvie Jr. and his wife, Velva Lyons, moved to Texas and started a traveling sales wagon, using loud speakers, to promote the elixir. The family divided the territory, and Rose Marie and Rhynhart took the Northwest, which led them up to Vancouver, British Columbia, Canada.

Life with Garreth in Vancouver was very turbulent. As a "speed artist," he would paint landscapes in the downtown department store windows while Rose Marie, standing nearby, would promote the elixir. Garreth did not handle money well, and he was heavily in debt. Her life traveling with him was a nightmare of evading police because of bad checks written in towns to which he never expected to return. Garreth also expected Rose Marie to cut all ties with her family; because of his possessive nature, Marie could only write to her daughter using another name. Although Rose Marie had always desired a large home and family, she lived in fear that she would bring a child into these unhappy circumstances.

At last, even though Garreth and Rose Marie finally established a small home, attended church, and even helped with the redecorating of the chapel there, Rose Marie knew she could not spend the rest of her life with a man she did not love. She made the very difficult decision to seek a divorce. Divorce in Canada was difficult to obtain; because she had dual citizenship in Canada and the United States, she decided to travel back to Boise to live with family members until the divorce in the American courts was final.

The marriage ended in the early summer of 1935, and Rose Marie returned to live in Vancouver, where Garreth still lived. Despite the divorce, Garreth remained her friend for several years, even during their subsequent marriages to other spouses. As the years passed, Rose Marie did not speak of her first marriage at all; her children considered Garreth a family friend and did not know of her true relationship with him until they were older. She never wanted any discussion of her years with Garreth to cause her to relive the memory of a marriage born of her concern for her family's welfare rather than love.

In 1938 Elvie Sr. was diagnosed with terminal cancer. For three excruciating years, Marie watched the sweetheart of her youth and the powerful father of her family deteriorate before her eyes. Before he died, he tried desperately to build Marie a second house to give her some rental property to help with her support. To work on the house, Elvie swung from one beam to the next on ropes so he would not have to climb on his swollen and painful legs. But his strength dwindled rapidly, and the house was never completed.

When Elvie could bear the pain no longer, Marie called their stake president (the ecclesiastical leader over the region). Kneeling at Elvie's bedside, together they prayed to God to release Elvie from his suffering. Elvie Sr. died minutes later. As she had not been able to when Oliver died, this time Marie did cry, and she cried the rest of her life. She always spoke of him as though he were near her, for in her heart he always was.

Even in death, Elvie Sr. continued to care for his family. Marion vividly recalled how some fifteen years after Elvie's death, she and Marie, along with Marion's children, were traveling home from California to Boise, Idaho. Marion was driving and the long distance exhausted her. As they drove into Elvie Jr.'s driveway, Marion suddenly awakened and said, "Oh, Mother, I must have been sound asleep! I don't remember anything since Marsing" (a town forty miles outside Boise). From her place in the back seat of the car, Marie responded softly, "I know, Marion. Daddy has been driving the car. He was right over your shoulder and he got us here safely."[8]

Notes

1. Rose Marie Reid, letter to Ruth Keller, 17 July 1954.
2. Marion Heilner and Elvie Yancey, interviews.
3. Marion Heilner, interview.
4. Weiser, Idaho, newspaper, 3 September 1925.
5. Rose Marie Reid, Divorce Summary, p. 2. This is a typed document in the possession of the authors.
6. Ibid.
7. Ibid.
8. Marion Heilner, interview.

Rose Marie Yancey

Jack C. Reid

CHAPTER 4

Reid Holiday Togs, Inc.

Divorced was a difficult label to wear in the 1930s, especially for a member of the Mormon Church. Elvie Sr. had been particularly disappointed in Rose Marie's divorce. Despite his sensitivity in so many ways, Elvie had always considered divorced people to be "secondhand goods," and Rose Marie knew this. Leaving behind the feelings of disapproval from her associates and family, Rose Marie left Idaho and returned to Vancouver where, for the first time in her life, she took time to do a few enjoyable things for herself. She had learned to play golf in Idaho, and now in Vancouver, she started taking swimming lessons at the Crystal Pool, where she met Jack C. Reid.

Jack Reid was the handsome, athletic manager and swimming instructor. Under his coaching she learned to swim well. She also learned what it felt like to experience feelings of romantic love. In return, Jack was attracted to her beauty and determination.

When Rose Marie first wrote to her family about Jack, they were skeptical. Their first concern was that he was not a member of her faith. But Jack was going to be baptized a member of the Church, Rose assured them, and when they felt her excitement, they became happy for her. To her dear sister, Rose Marie wrote, "Oh Marion, he's so much fun and so smart."[1]

Like Rose Marie, Jack had been married before but was

divorced. He had one child. Like Rose, Jack shared the label of "secondhand goods." Now they could have a second chance. They would have a family and a life together. Their marriage took place on 30 November 1935.

The young couple lived for a while in Jack's apartment over the swimming pool, where they were extremely happy. Rose Marie displayed her talents decorating their little home and making it comfortable. Neither had any idea that their lives were about to change dramatically.

Swimming attire in the 1930s consisted solely of heavy wool trunks for men and tank suits for women. While a person was swimming, the water would soak into the fabric, making it unsightly and uncomfortable. In fact, the suit was a detriment to the serious swimmer. Jack disliked his own swimsuits, so Rose Marie simply took fabric from an old duck coat and sewed a well-fitted suit with laces up the side. It was a remarkable improvement, and those who came to the pool asked where they could get a suit like his. Jack saw an opportunity to supplement their income and the possibility of a very successful business.

Rose Marie had no such aspirations. In fact, she was weary of business. Years later, in her oral history, she admitted, "I didn't want to have anything to do with business because I'd had enough of it, but my husband wanted it and insisted we take this opportunity."[2] Even Marie, Rose's mother, who was visiting, encouraged her to make a few suits: "Maybe they won't be any good and then you'll be through with the subject, so why not do it?"

So Rose Marie made a duplicate suit, and Jack took it to the Hudson Bay Department Store. "Does your company make ladies' suits as well?" he was asked. Although there was as yet no company, Jack answered in the affirmative. When he returned home, he told Rose Marie that the buyers would be coming in a week, and they wanted to see a lady's suit.

Rose Marie was so troubled and frightened at the prospect that she knelt in prayer that very evening and poured out her heart. God knew that her greatest desire was to be a mother and raise children. If He wanted her to make bathing suits, it was up to Him; He would have to arrange things. The next day, using a lovelier fabric, she was able to make a woman's swimsuit, again with laces up the side. When the buyers came, they ordered ten dozen men's and six dozen ladies' suits. Said Rose, "The Lord must have wanted [the buyers] to have the suits."[3] Reid's Holiday Togs, Ltd., was born.

Rose Marie knew nothing of manufacturing. She thought at first that she would just design the suits and have a manufacturer make them. But no one wanted anything to do with such a small order. So Rose Marie, using her Yancey ingenuity, called the Singer Sewing Machine Company to obtain the names of sixteen women who had purchased sewing machines in her area, then contracted them to sew for her in their homes. The first season, the local business inspector allowed her to have the suits made in private homes. They sold wonderfully well, and she grossed $10,000.

The next year, however, neither the inspectors nor the city would let her continue this arrangement. They insisted that the company be under one roof. So Rose Marie rented a building and sixteen machines, and expanded the number to thirty-two within a month.

Operating capital was the greatest obstacle to the young company. It was just before World War II, and few wanted to invest in a venture so small and so tenuous. The first two years, Rose Marie had to pay eighteen percent interest on the borrowed money. When she asked for a reduced rate the third year, one of the men said, "If you think you can get money somewhere cheaper than this, well, do it!" So she did![4]

As Rose Marie began to see all the possibilities to improve the fit of swimsuits, her innate creativity soared. In the first year, Rose Marie designed only six different styles; she later expanded to over one hundred different styles in a single season. Occasionally she sketched designs as she thought of them, but she always did her real designing on live models.

Rose Marie noticed that many women were self-conscious about appearing in swimming attire. The suits sagged from the weight of the water, and the women often felt immodest and unattractive so many refused to swim. Rose Marie saw the necessity of developing the capabilities of fabric so that swimsuits would retain their shape when wet. Up to this time, beautiful fabrics had never even been considered for swimwear. She began using gabardine and cotton,

One of the "Canadian print" collection of 1941.
It was considered the pride of the Northwest.

Models show mother and daughter Skintite suits.
Toddler Sharon Reid stands at right.

lacing them for fit. In time, the lace-down suits became very popular and stylish. Zippers were difficult to obtain because of the war; they also invited rust. Most important, Rose Marie's riveting machines had been so expensive that she could not afford *not* to use them.

Rose Marie was the first to use inside brassieres, tummy-tuck panels, stay-down legs, and laces. These innovative features made her suits very popular. She also designed matching mother-daughter swimsuits as well as suits for men, boys, and children of all ages. She was the first to introduce dress sizes in swimwear. She also began to think of ladies with larger figures, building foundation garments (for control) within the suits.[5]

Her philosophy was to make a swimsuit that would make women feel as lovely wearing it as they would feel wearing a ballroom gown.

The business grew rapidly. In one season, sales went from $30,000 to $300,000. Her designs became so popular that they were used by women participants in the 1937 British Empire Games in Australia. The company's products were sold throughout Canada in more than five hundred retail stores. Annual sales grew from $32,000 in 1938 to $834,000 in 1946. By 1946, Rose Marie Reid would capture about 50 percent of the swimsuit market in Canada.[6]

During an interview for a Vancouver newspaper, Fred MacGregor of Spencer's Department Store recalled the first day he met Rose Marie. She had taken a few samples of her swimsuits to his store to see whether he would carry them. "He remembered that he had $10,000 worth of ladies' bathing suits and was all set for summer . . . . He looked at the samples and he made a dubious face, but being a good sport he gave her an order anyway."[7] Later, he took Rose Marie's suits off the counter and hid them, because people came in and insisted that he get more of them before he could sell his other swimsuits. Before the summer ended, he had sold more than five thousand of her suits.

At one time, Rose Marie began a traveling fashion show to propel her designs into the spotlight. The show, "Out of the West," featured a long pier with a diving board. She "paraded her Powers" down a long pier in black satin buckskins and bright prints. Some of the designs featured the first built-in corsets. She also featured a unique Canadian print that had totem poles instead of the usual fish, and tepees and snowshoes instead of Hawaiian palm trees. Other prints featured Quebec scenes with oxcarts, maple trees with their sap buckets, outdoor bake ovens, log cabins, and spinning wheels spiked with a scattering of *fleur de lis* and the provincial crest. Her genius won her praise as "Canada's best-known designer."[8] Almost sixty years after she first began designing, Canadians would still refer to her as their native-born product, their national treasure.[9]

The *Vancouver Daily Province* gave Rose Marie Reid the title "Vancouver's famous swimsuit maker," and featured Rose Marie's suits.[10]

Rose Marie wanted, even felt she needed to move the company to Montreal. She learned that Beatrice Pines Bathing Suits was copying her designs. The water lily and dragon-fly design Rose Marie had hand painted began appearing on Beatrice Pines' suits, and the only way Rose Marie could cope with such blatant theft was to be in Montreal daily.

Benefiting from its prime location in Montreal, Beatrice Pines Bathing Suits had also been able to obtain special concessions from the fabric companies, circumventing the existing quotas imposed by the Wage Price Board, who regulated the wartime economy. On the other hand, Rose Marie had been held to a 1941 quota. Pines had even gone to the paint manufacturer, who had promised Rose Marie an exclusive on the special paint used in the design, and bought Rose Marie's exclusive paint. Because Pines was there "on the ground," close to all the big markets and fabric producers, their suits could be painted within a week and photographs quickly taken. Their advertisements would come out two months ahead of Rose Marie's, and thus make it appear that Rose Marie's was the copy instead of the original.[11]

However, Rose Marie was hindered by her financiers, E. J. Meilicke and his brother, who, together with Rose Marie and Jack, owned all the stock in the Canadian enterprise. Insisting that they be involved in all aspects of the company, the Meilickes became more of an obstacle than a help. They could not understand Rose

Marie's predicament, and they would not let her move, nor would they let her buy their position in the company. To her request for relocation, E. L. Meilecke sent a terse paragraph-by-paragraph reply: "We do not agree that we must manufacture in Montreal immediately. . . . We regard your offer to buy our stock as an attempt to gain voting control."[12]

Meilicke demanded that Rose Marie specify her reasons for the need to make the move in writing, even though they had discussed these reasons many times face-to-face. She responded, "I will not trust anyone else to be there and make the decisions for me. . . . This business has been built on my ability to see things that other people missed, and that is still my only hope of survival. Competitors will be copying my things so much that I can never dare to make 'run-of-the-mill' things."[13]

Although the Meilickes' services consisted mainly of signing checks to pay for wages and materials, they insisted on absolute control of the operation in addition to compensation for the power they exercised. In response to their financial demands, Rose Marie complained, "Anything beyond bank interest on loans plus a reasonable bonus plus a pro rata share of profits is all that a silent financial partner can expect. The $2400 per year for signing cheques and very light services should be adequate but you favor more."[14]

Rose Marie's swimsuits would have made their international plunge seven or eight years earlier had it not been for the Meilicke brothers, as all design and sales decisions were influenced by them. A review of the written correspondence between Rose Marie and E. J. Meilicke reveals how the plodding financier can frustrate the genuine creator. (Most of Rose Marie's letters to the Meilickes are undated and typed on the back of old invoices. The invoices, however, are dated, and they have become invaluable links in the sequence of events.)

Another obstacle encountered by Rose Marie was the difficulty in obtaining fabric. The War Department had placed all fabric mills on restrictions and quotas. This led to an active black market. Rose Marie was very active in developing specialized fabrics for swimwear. Lastex, Lurex, and brocaded satins were part of her genius. To Meilicke she complained, "I saw my exclusive satin, made by another mill, at a time when mills are not supposed to make any new cloths."[15] And in New York she was told that no cotton would be available. It was only an old manufacturing friend that saved her from bankruptcy. "You go to Charlie Northcott in Toronto," he told Rose Marie, "and tell him I said to let you have some of our cottons."[16]

The Meilickes also objected to Jack receiving a commission for his sales made after hours. (He was then receiving $3,600 per year as advertising and promotions manager.) Rose Marie tried valiantly to get Jack's salary equal to hers (she was paid $7,500 as designer), insisting to the Meilickes that Jack should be paid more. "[The extra sales are] only made possible by Jack giving not eight but twelve to sixteen hours a day to the business," she told the Meilickes. "Likewise if it is possible to take on more territory and cover it adequately either with or without subordinate help, we should be allowed to benefit by it, so long as the cost to the company is not increased."[17] The Meilickes insisted on value, however, and they were not about to pay Jack the same wage for advertising and promotion as they paid the heart, soul, and brains of the company.

The difference between Rose Marie and Jack's salaries was only one cause of friction between them. Rose Marie's persuasive personality and charm made her approach much more appealing than Jack's imperious and dictatorial style, and lenders refused to deal with him. This fact threatened her relationship with Jack, and Rose Marie found herself caught in an impossible situation. Jack not only insisted that she work, but drove her to keep working. He had assured her that if she would help him in this business, he would handle the business and she would be free to design. But it was not to be.

Rose Marie had also expected that her efforts would enable him to discontinue his work at the Crystal Pool. However, Jack kept up his pool connections—with suspiciously late hours—and left Rose Marie to manage the company. "I had known when I married Jack that he was ambitious. I admired him for it in contrast to my first marriage," Rose Marie wrote. "I thought I was keeping peace to make the first swimsuit. I was badly mistaken. . . . I learned now that Jack's ambition took the form of keeping other people working. With never a let up and no matter how much they did, it was never enough to get a word of praise nor gratitude, only fault-finding and complaints at every slight mistake."[18]

Rose Marie also told Marion how desperately she wanted children, but Jack had made it very clear that these were not his desires. Doctors informed her that she needed minor surgery and some medication to correct her physical inability to conceive. She had the surgery, and just after the birth of Sanford Jr., Marion's second child, Rose Marie excitedly wrote Marion that she, too, was pregnant.

Jack was furious and insisted that she continue to work. She worked so hard, in fact, that she nearly lost the baby. Even when she got to the hospital, said Marion, Rose Marie "was still cutting and designing right on the hospital bed. Jack didn't want her to stop for a minute."

Bruce Alan Reid was born 19 January 1937. With the birth of her first child, Rose Marie was ecstatic. "She loved being pregnant more than any other woman I've ever known," said Marion. Rose Marie had an amazingly high pain threshold. She told her daughter Carole that having a baby didn't hurt a bit (which Carole believed until she had her own first baby). Carole decided that her mother "was just so exhausted from working so hard" that she was happy to "finally have a chance to sleep." Bruce's birth left Rose Marie's arm paralyzed for three months; despite her tolerance for pain, she found it necessary to take painkillers.

Obsessed with keeping the business growing, Jack was furious at any delay in the work. Rose Marie scrambled to fill orders, getting up each morning at 4:00 a.m. to cut out suits. Despite her work, though, she always took time to bathe the baby herself. Watching her with their son, Jack accused Rose Marie of laziness. "You'd never do anything if I didn't force you," he told her angrily.[19] He did all the work, he said, but she got all the credit. At times his temper was uncontrollable. One day he smashed a rock crystal vase against a bookcase, all the while screaming his rage at her. Rose Marie ran for the bedroom door, but she couldn't close the door in time. Grabbing a chair, Jack smashed it against her side and Rose crumpled to the bed. He continued to beat the chair against the floor until it fractured into splinters. Hearing the ruckus, workers below ran upstairs; but, fearful of Jack, they backed away. One worker later told Rose

Marie, "If you don't stand up to Jack, he'll kill you."[20]

Marie was no silent witness in the face of Jack's cruelty to her daughter. Mother and daughter often worked on the swimsuits long hours into the night at Rose Marie's home, and Marie described to Marion how she once told Jack, "If you ever strike her again, I'll kill you."[21] To see her daughter endure such pain was too much for her.

Rose Marie felt that if she divorced Jack, she would never have the opportunity to have more children, which she wanted desperately. Her work, she decided, would be her salvation, and she threw herself into it. At one point Jack even restricted her from using the car, but she was determined to patiently work out their problems, praying somehow that their marriage would improve and she would have more children.

It was not long before she was again pregnant. Again she was thrilled, and again Jack was furious. For him, one baby was enough; two was an outrage. Rose Marie assured him, however, that she would manage so well he would never see a difference. Jack held her to that promise.

When she was ready to deliver the baby, Rose Marie was alone. It was 2:00 a.m., and she couldn't find Jack anywhere. She expected her friend and Bruce's babysitter, Mommy Wood, to come in the morning, so she waited, holding back the birth. On her arrival, Mommy Wood rushed Rose Marie to the hospital. Rose Marie was so exhausted that she nearly slept through the entire birth.

Sharon was born 2 October 1938. When Sharon was old enough to understand, Rose Marie would tell her daughter, "I prayed all night, with every labor pain, that I could wait until Mommy Wood could come to help me and take care of Bruce."

Once again Rose Marie was quickly back at work, conducting business and creating designs from her hospital bed. Salesmen, cutters, models, and materials crowded her room from 8:00 a.m. to 9:00 p.m.

Notes

1. Marion Heilner, interview.
2. Rose Marie Reid, Oral History, p. 44.
3. Ibid., p. 45.

4. Ibid., p. 46.

5. *San Francisco Examiner,* 8 May 1950.

6. Tax Court of the United States, Docket No. 51225, Filed 21 June 1956, p. 623.

7. *Vancouver Daily Province,* 22 January 1949.

8. *Globe and Mail,* 13 December 1945, p.13.

9. Bosker, Gideon, and Lena Lencek, "In the Swim," *Alaska Airlines,* January 1990, p. 31.

10. *Vancouver Daily Province,* 22 January 1949.

11. Rose Marie Reid, letter to E. L. Meilicke, n.d. (Rose Marie's letters were written on the back of invoices for cloth fabrics; not all invoice dates were legible. Also, Rose Marie did not write internal dates on her letters.)

12. E. L. Meilicke, letter to Reid's Holiday Togs, 2 May 1944.

13. Rose Marie Reid, letter to E. L. Meilicke, n.d.

14. Rose Marie Reid, letter to E. L. Meilicke, n.d.

15. Rose Marie Reid, letter to E. L. Meilicke, n.d.

16. E. L. Meilicke, letter to Rose Marie Reid, n.d.

17. Rose Marie Reid, letter to E. L. Meilicke (the invoice on which it was written is dated 29 April 1942).

18. Rose Marie Reid, Divorce Summary, p. 4.

19. Ibid., p. 5.

20. Ibid., p. 4.

21. Ibid., p. 7.

Rose Marie with children Sharon, Carole, and Bruce.

Windows in Spencer's Department Store in Vancouver. Sharon (two years old) models her mother's suit. Rose Marie stands at far right.

CHAPTER 5

Working Mother

From 1938 to 1944, the company's staff grew from 2 to 190 employees. The business was growing so rapidly that Rose Marie was needed there constantly, and since she'd struggled so hard to have her babies, she wanted them with her every minute. Rose Marie began taking them to the plant with her; when she was nursing Sharon, she kept a playpen under the design table. Jack accused Rose Marie of willfully neglecting business just to be with her children, although Rose Marie worked around the clock. She even took Sharon with her on buying trips to New York, and her baby had the distinction of being the youngest baby to fly across the country before 1938. The New York newspapers made a great fuss over the flight.

Marion recounts how Rose Marie brought six-week-old Sharon with her on a major buying and selling trip to New York. Rose conducted business in one room of her two-room suite at the Plaza Hotel, and reserved the other for her new baby and herself. When buyers met with her, she would always take them in to see her baby first. By the time they were ready to talk business, any formality between buyer and seller had been transformed to warm friendship. Said one competitor, "I can compete with her swimsuits, and with her selling ability, but I cannot compete with that baby."[1]

When first interviewed by the *Vancouver Sun*, Rose Marie was the mother of only one child, her son, Bruce. "Bruce is the first of six," she told them smiling.[2]

She often put in sixteen-hour days. She commuted between Vancouver and Montreal, and to New York, Los Angeles, Miami, Baltimore, and Chicago. Rose Marie greatly regretted being away from her young family, but it was the only way she could do what had to be done.

The children always knew they had access to their mother by phone and letter. She lived for their letters and checked at each hotel for even a short, poorly scribbled note. In her letters she expressed her love for them and taught them of spiritual things. She reminded them to say their prayers and always to be helpful to their grandma.

As business grew, Rose Marie began to look in earnest for fabrics that did new and different things for women. Bengaline, satin brocade, beautiful trims, braids, and embroideries—all became beautifully fashioned swimwear. A lobster was placed on one model of glistening white. On another there were fish with sparkling little mirrors. Her best seller of that season was a fabric called "plastylon," mixing the qualities of plastic and nylon.[3]

Rose Marie was pregnant with Bruce while she was working on the "Skintite" line. She was so self-conscious that pictures from this era show her designing on beautiful models, but her own tummy is carefully penciled out so no one can see the slight bulge. A war-time photo of the Skintite featured this patriotic paragraph: "Because we feel that they are one of the finest collections of swimsuits ever created in Canada, we are pleased to devote a large part of our space in the *Bruck Fabric News* to the Skintite Swim Suits." The magazine went on to inform the readers that Mrs. Reid's suits met all the wartime regulations, and ended with the epithet: "Pay your taxes and beat the Ax[-]is!"[4] Jack added a marketing promotion by offering four free swimming lessons at the Crystal Pool to anyone who purchased a suit. Yvonne De Carlo, a promising young Hollywood movie star, chose one of Rose Marie's suits for a promotional shot, both women being from Canada. And Janet Blair, another Hollywood star, used one of her suits in a national advertisement for Lucky Strike cigarettes.

The secret to the Skintite was a one-inch band of fabric around the back and up over the shoulder. The suit fit snugly into place, holding firmly to the woman's figure during even the most strenuous beach activity. Rose Marie believed that for a woman to be comfortable, she had to be covered up in the right places. "Nothing is so brutally frank as the bare essentials of a bathing suit," said Rose Marie.[5] Quality control was her trademark; her suits were always given exhaustive tests before going on the market. One test was with the Canadian Coast Guard girls, asking them to "go hard on [the suits]. Only if the suits survived a month of this treatment were they put on the production line."[6]

Spencer's Department Store created a window display featuring the Skintite suits. In the window was a large tank into which a man and a woman dived and swam in full view of the public. This display caused a stir, and crowds blocked traffic to see it. Rose Marie's children were also used as live models in the windows of the Hudson Bay store, where they played all day in a sandbox. Every few hours the store would change their suits and send them into the large windows, modeling for all the window shoppers of downtown Vancouver.

Rose Marie had been married to Jack barely five years when it became evident to her that her second marriage, like her first, was doomed to failure. Believing that this would be her final marriage and her last opportunity for children, she carefully planned the conception and birth of her last child, Carole Marie Reid. She was thrilled when her third child was born 18 July 1940.

Rose Marie realized that her husband had joined the Mormon Church without real commitment or testimony. Evidently from the beginning he had had no intention of living its precepts. Rose Marie had been optimistic about his acceptance of the Church, but he was far from her spiritual equal, and his physical violence destined the marriage for destruction. Workers from the plant and at the pool tried to help Rose Marie, but a broken arm and numerous bruises bore visible witness to Jack's cruelty. Marie, Marion, and even Jack's own mother acknowledged his abuse. Bruce remembered cowering in the corner with Sharon in fear of their father.[7] Bruce had experienced his father's violent nature when Jack thrust Bruce's hand into a furnace, severely burning it, as punishment for playing with matches.

The Meilickes were very concerned about the discord in the marriage. At one point, E. L. Meilicke said to Jack: "I cannot understand what kind of a creature you are. It seems to me that any man in the world would be proud and so thankful that he had a wife like yours that he would do everything in his power to make things easy for her; look what she has done for you. She is a wife in every sense of the word. You have both told us that never at any time has she refused to cohabit with you, even at times when you had just during the day been violently cruel to her. She has borne you three beautiful children and manages to keep a house that any man would be proud of if it was his wife's full-time job. Then besides all that, through her own ability to design and conduct business, she has set you up in the very business that allows you to manage, to advance as far as you are capable. . . . [The business] has unlimited possibilities. Every store in Canada and her business associates are commending what she has done, yet you hound the life out of her as though she was a personal slave who never did anything. You keep her in such an upset mental condition that she is going to break one of these days."[8]

Rose Marie tried two different separations from Jack, but all efforts at reconciliation proved futile. Jack made promises but quickly broke them.

Rose Marie was near complete mental collapse when she visited a lawyer, who told her that adultery was the only cause for which a divorce was granted. Rose Marie knew of her husband's unfaithfulness, but was reluctant to engage in a long, drawn-out legal battle. The lawyer suggested that there was an alternative, but he doubted she would be interested. Rose Marie was desperate, and willing to consider anything to put an end to her painful relationship with Jack.

The lawyer told her that, in reality, since her Idaho divorce from Garreth Rynhart was not valid in Canada, she could obtain an annulment from Jack on that basis. Rose Marie saw this as the escape she sought, and her marriage to Jack Reid was annulled based on the fact that she had been legally married to Garreth Rynhart at the time. This, she knew, would leave her virtually defenseless as far as property was concerned; any property settlement would go in Jack's favor since she would be deemed at fault. Most significant, such action would make her children illegitimate in the eyes of the law. Nevertheless, Rose Marie chose this route as the simplest, kindest way to free herself and protect her children from Jack, as he would have no legal claim upon them.

The decree was issued 10 April 1946: "This court doth order and decree that the marriage entered into between the petitioner [Rose Marie] and the Respondent [Jack Reid]. . . is hereby declared to be null and void and of no effect by reason of a prior marriage then existing between the Petitioner, then known as Rose Marie Rynhart."⁹ The court showed its sympathy with Rose Marie by ordering Jack to pay the costs incident to the trial.

Rose Marie's problems, however, were not at an end. In order to own the company outright, she had to buy Jack's interest, for which he asked an exorbitant price. Jack also took $80,000 worth of fabric from the factory without consulting Rose Marie.¹⁰

Taking the money, Jack moved to the beaches of North Vancouver and built a large, spacious home with lovely grounds and a swimming pool extending over the ocean. Within a few weeks after the annulment, he married Rose Marie's best friend.

When Jack began playing the extravagant father with Bruce, showering him with trips and gifts, Rose Marie responded in a letter, "Quit laying it on thick with Bruce, please," she wrote. "I know that you do not care how hard you make it for me, but do not make it hard for him, which is what you will do. You are rich and free and I am in debt to the point of drudgery for the next ten years, so I will never be able to compete with you in either time nor money that you can lavish on him. . . . Your last move [stealing the fabric] has tied me hand and foot to business all the rest of Bruce's childhood."¹¹

Before Rose Marie left Vancouver, Jack's final insult was to steal half of the little house she had purchased from the railroad for $3,000, a house she had bought out of her earnings and furnished with boxes and discarded furniture. The carpets she had obtained from the old Heilner mansion belonging to Marion's in-laws in Baker, Oregon. Jack had neither paid a dime nor driven a nail in the improvement of the house. Rose Marie wrote to Marion: "I am so mad I could chew nails. I had the lawyer phone J. C. [Jack] and tell him that I wanted him to sign the deed to the house. It is in both names, fool that I was. I had explained to the lawyer that the only money he could ever have been construed to have paid on it was the loan on his insurance, for $360. But . . . I had had the house put in both names, hoping that it would make him have a more 'family feeling.'"[12]

In contrast, Garreth wrote to her when she left for Los Angeles: "Dear Roses . . . , I write many letters to you but they never get on paper. But this one will. The early morning hours are always yours. (It's 5 a.m.). . . . We miss you Roses. . . . I am sad for the want of you and now you're sure to go out of my life forever."[13] Although Garreth was happily married with a young daughter, he remembered with fondness the loveliness Rose Marie had once brought to his life.

The annulment was financially devastating for Rose Marie, and she searched for ways to bring in extra income for the company. Her ten-year-old daughter, Sharon, suggested that she make housecoats for women. Canada had all the housecoat manufacturers it needed, but Rose Marie felt she could contribute something new, something no one else was doing. She told her daughters to pray for this success, and then began asking questions of a hundred women—girls in offices, women in the factory, wives, and church friends. All agreed they wanted something a little glamorous, and they didn't want wool.

To meet this demand, an entirely new fabric had to be created. Mr. Binz, owner of the only company capable of making such a fabric, said that he had "no time for specialty things." But Rose Marie literally charmed him into trying. They worked together, and within one week had created two perfect fabrics. New names were needed for them, so Rose Marie honored the two children who were at home praying for the project by calling them "Sharonel" and "Carolecord." The girls prayed hard, and the debt for which the line was created was paid in less than a year. The housecoats only lasted for a few years, but they generated the necessary income to see Rose Marie through this difficult time.

Notes

1. Marion Heilner, unpublished biography of Rose Marie Reid, 1951.
2. *Vancouver Sun*, n.d.
3. *Toronto Evening Telegram*, 7 December 1944.
4. *Bruck Fabric News*, vol. 4, no. 1, January/February 1943.
5. *New Liberty*, 21 February 1948, pp. 14-15.
6. Ibid.
7. Bruce Reid, letter to Carole Burr and Sharon Alden, n.d.
8. E. L. Meilicke, as quoted in Rose Marie Reid's Divorce Summary, p. 9.
9. Supreme Court of British Columbia, N. 1658/45.
10. Rose Marie Reid, letter to Marion Heilner, n.d.
11. Rose Marie Reid, letter to Jack Reid, n.d.
12. Rose Marie Reid, letter to Marion Heilner, 19 February 1949.
13. Garreth Rhynhart, letter to Rose Marie Reid, 25 May 1949.

Rose Marie places her handprint on the cement at her new factory on Century Boulevard in Los Angeles.

Rose Marie Reid factory at 5200 West Century Boulevard. Erected on a three and a half acres, the factory held 65,000 square feet of work space.

CHAPTER 6

California

It had been obvious to Rose Marie for some time that her only
real future or hope for her children was to somehow move them to
the United States. As early as 1938, she had begun making the
attempt to enter the United States' markets, licensing her name and
her patents to a Baltimore, Maryland, firm that sold the products
nationally and internationally under the trade name "Rose Marie
Reid." In November 1938, the *Vancouver Sun* pictured Rose Marie
arriving in Vancouver on a United Air Lines flight. The accompanying article states:

> Mrs. Jack Reid, 564 West Broadway, young Vancouver
> mother, who made a pair of swimming trunks for her
> husband and revolutionized the bathing suit industry,
> arrived home Saturday from a business trip to Baltimore
> with the United States tucked in her pocket. The Reid
> "Skintite" will be seen in the future at all America's
> smartest bathing beaches. Bests of New York are handling
> them and Mrs. Reid flew to Baltimore to confer with the
> company's representatives. The suits will be manufactured
> in the United States.
> "They told me it was the most brilliant idea in years,"
> said Mrs. Reid. . . . The suit took on so rapidly that from

having a few girls work at home, the Reids started a factory. Recently it has been on double shift.

"It's a grand business, for it's always summer and swim time somewhere," said Mrs. Reid. "We shipped 3,000 suits to Australia last week."

"Now we've a new bright idea: swim suits that don't get wet. We call it 'Zelan' and we've patented the idea. The suits will be made in light-weight cotton or satin, unstretchable, cut to hold the shape, body-fitting and color fast. Our only worry is they'll last forever," said Mrs. Reid.[1]

Rose Marie was to receive a royalty of ten percent of the Baltimore sales, which netted her $11,000 in 1938. However, because of the difficulty of traveling between Baltimore and Vancouver and managing business over such long distances, the venture was closed after only one year.

Eight years later, in 1946, Mr. Mcgregor of Spencer's Department Store introduced Rose Marie to Jack Kessler, a distributor for White Stagg and a representative for Louis Tabak and Company located in Burbank, California. Having brought two of her swimsuits with her to the luncheon, Rose Marie presented them to Kessler to take home to his wife, Nina. Nina loved them. She had just had a baby, and found the suits' fit and support to be wonderful.

Kessler showed great interest in Rose Marie's designs, and Rose Marie expressed her plans to move into the United States. She was looking for the right opportunity, she told him.

Fascinated with her talent, Kessler discussed such an opportunity with Louis Tabak, who discouraged the idea because four large, established companies—Jantzen, Catalina, Cole, and Mabs—completely dominated the American market. A further difficulty was that postwar shortages made it difficult for new ventures.

Kessler told Rose Marie that Tabak had said a new swimsuit business in the United States was impossible. But Rose Marie was not one to give up. Nina Kessler later said that Rose Marie's attitude was "If you could think of it, you could do it. If any other person could do it, then there wasn't any reason why she couldn't. [And] she could do it better."² Attributing his own success to the pace Rose Marie set, Jack Kessler agreed that Rose Marie was the strongest-willed person he'd ever known. She was willing to work twice as long and hard as anyone else in the industry, he said.

Later that same year, Rose Marie approached Jack and Nina Kessler a second time, asking them to go into business with her. But Kessler was comfortable in his job and his home in Seattle. The Kesslers lived comfortably with their four children in a big house in Seattle, and they had a lovely summer home on an island in Puget Sound. Louis Tabak's advice still seemed sound to him: "Forget it, Jack! You can't get the machines, you can't get fabric, you can't get a place. You can't even get help." Remembering this, Kessler put Rose Marie off. "If you could get the machines and the fabric and the help, we could do it," he told her, thinking it such an impossible task that she would certainly fail and that would be the end of it.

But he did not know Rose Marie. Within days, he was awakened by a 4:30 a.m. phone call from Rose Marie. "I've got everything lined up," she announced. Kessler was slow to remember his words to Rose Marie. Confused and very conscious of his seven-person party line and all of his uninvited listeners, he said, "What have you got lined up?"

"I've got the machines—and the fabric!" she said. Still sleepy and bemused, Kessler responded, "I'll call you back later."

He talked to his wife Nina, who despite Tabak's advice said, "If we hitch our wagon to that young woman, we'll go places." In an interview for *This Week* magazine, Nina described how Jack was "fearful of the new venture." She said to him, "Just wait until women start wearing Rose Marie Reid suits. We won't be able to make them fast enough."³

The Kesslers met Rose Marie in New York. She invited the Kesslers to her hotel room, where she had fabrics in the bathtub and all over the furniture. "She was the most organized, unorganized person I knew," said Nina. She was absolutely fearless, and she did what had to be done immediately, no matter what anybody thought. Nina recalled a time soon after Rose Marie had given birth to Sharon, when she was meeting with a group of executives in Baltimore. "During the meeting, Sharon became hungry and started crying, and Rose Marie just put the baby blanket over her blouse and started breast-feeding the baby right there," said Nina. "This was so typically Rose Marie Reid. I don't know anyone else who would have done it."

In response to Kessler's challenge, Rose Marie had arranged for forty sewing machines from the Singer Company in Winnipeg, Canada. The Singer representative in New York couldn't believe she had done it. Kessler said, "She knew how to handle such people. She would get all their attention, and she'd somehow get them to [do] the impossible."

Rose Marie had contacted the Singer company and requested forty machines. Her name would be placed on a waiting list, she was told. She grew impatient waiting, and one morning she got up, packed, and went to Winnepeg, where she told the Singer distributor that she had come for her machines.

Appalled, the distributor told her she shouldn't have wasted her time coming there. They hadn't notified her to come, and the waiting list was very long.

"I know you have the machines, and I'll wait," she replied. Within hours, a company that had closed down returned their machines. When the distributor received this information, he could hardly believe it. It was exactly the number Rose Marie had ordered. Because she was there, he gave her the machines. "I can't ever remember her telling anyone how she knew about those machines," mused her daughter Sharon.

Even though there was as yet no formal corporation formed, Rose Marie told Kessler to call Louis Tabak and see if he would hold the machines at his company until they could get to Los Angeles.

What do you mean you have the machines?" was Tabak's response.

"We've got machines and fabric," Kessler told him.

"Jack, you're nuts!" Tabak protested. Nevertheless, Tabak was willing to hold the machines. If the new company failed, he would buy the machines and give Rose Marie and Kessler a good profit on them. Tabak's eagerness to get the machines from them scared both Kessler and Rose Marie, but they determined he would never get them.

Jack and Nina returned immediately to Seattle and began selling

(From left to right) Manager Henry Kessler, Nina and Jack Kessler, and Rose Marie

their home and properties in order to raise money. They had promised to front the company with $50,000. This figure later became the subject of a court battle, although throughout her life Rose Marie always acknowledged, in speeches and privately, that it took great courage for the Kesslers to leave their secure family setting and venture with an unknown. "They had faith in my ability, and I had enough faith in God for both of us," she said gratefully.

When they arrived in Los Angeles, Nina and Jack bought a duplex in Beverly Hillls, which for a time became their home and office. Rose Marie arrived a few days later with four models from Canada. Together with Jack and Nina, they found a warehouse in downtown Los Angeles on Santee Street. Although it was in one of the worst areas of Los Angeles, it had a spacious upper floor. Even today, the streets are littered and the outside walls of the factory are covered with graffiti. Inside, immigrants from Taiwan still sew garments; outside, street vendors still sell their wares.

Rose Marie took up residence in the warehouse itself, living alone in the old warehouse for nearly two years until she could buy a home and bring her children from their home in Vancouver, where they were cared for alternately by Rose Marie's mother and a hired nanny.

By now her swimsuits had been featured in *Life* magazine, but

Rose Marie was still aware that penetrating the U.S. markets would be difficult, especially since the duty imposed by United States Customs made Rose Marie's suits twice as expensive as comparable U.S. lines. To overcome this handicap, she tenaciously searched for avenues to channel her swimsuits through. She knew of a wonderful and influential buyer named Marjorie Griswald from New York's Lord and Taylor Department Store. With determination, she was able to contact her. Rose Marie told her that she made suits uniquely different from the U.S. manufacturers and would like Marjorie to see them. Marjorie's reply was a miracle. She told Rose Marie she'd be right over, and she came to her hotel. Without even seeing the suits on models, she bought them.

It was the beginning of a long professional relationship and a valued personal friendship. They corresponded regularly, and Marjorie became a friend and confidant. "It was the Lord that impressed her to come to my hotel," Rose Marie always proclaimed.

Marjorie was pleased to describe the effect that Rose Marie Reid swimsuits had on the customer. As she stood in the store and watched, she saw people looking at different swimsuits. "They'd come back to [Rose Marie's], and . . . take it into the fitting room and then they would come to another suit of [hers]," taking several Rose Marie swimsuits into the fitting room with them. Marjorie concluded, "It was very interesting to see that just hanging on the rack . . . , those were the ones that [the women] would take into the fitting room with them."[4]

Marjorie was directly responsible for the success of Rose Marie's debut, although Rose Marie and the Kesslers were unaware of her role until after the show. Marjorie was a passenger on the train hired by Cole of California to travel from New York to Los Angeles. The train collected buyers across the country and brought them to California for the showing of Cole's new swimsuit line. Marjorie went through the train, recommending that the buyers also take time to see the line of a new young designer from Canada. Marjorie told them all about Rose Marie's innovative designs and her wonderful new style, gave them the address, and said, "Don't miss her show or you'll be sorry. You must meet Rose Marie Reid."[5]

In the meantime, prior to the show, Rose had developed a stunning new fabric for a swimsuit that would become enormously

Rose Marie wove the first metallic threads into fabric and designed a swimsuit that became a glamour item for movie stars and beauty queens.

popular. While in New York buying fabrics, she had noticed a roll of metal yarn on the desk of a fabric company executive. It was being used only for braids and trims. Rose Marie asked for a piece, took it back to her hotel, and dipped it in salt water, thinking that if the yarn didn't rust, she would have it woven into a fabric. When it didn't tarnish, she bought twenty yards each of the silver and gold yarn, took the thread to a weaver, and swore him to secrecy. She waited a couple of days and returned to find an exquisite gold and silver metallic fabric—the first of its kind! She picked up the yardage and took it with her to Los Angeles, where she revealed her plans to Jack Kessler. "It's pretty," said Kessler. But he thought no one would buy it.

Rose Marie was convinced otherwise. "It will sell," she said, and almost immediately began fitting the material on a model.

She worked night and day until she had created a selection of exquisite swimsuits. The debut of Rose Marie Reid, Inc., of

California took place in Los Angeles on 20 September 1946. Her fashion show was held at the factory on Santee Street. As she unveiled her new line, the feature and finale was her beautiful gold metallic suit. The suit sold for a whopping $90, when most swimsuits sold for $6.95.

When the time came for the show to begin, she still had unfinished suits that were supposed to be presented, so she brought her sewing machine into the dressing room. Said Nina, "Models [sat] there naked while [Rose Marie] worked to tighten a seam." When it came time to go out onto the floor, Rose Marie put on her own makeup as she prepared to narrate.

To everyone's complete astonishment, over one hundred people came to the showroom, filling the room to capacity. They held three showings a day.

"She came out with the 'Oh, we didn't have time to completely price the line,' and she got a tremendous reception," said Kessler. "They priced the line right during the show, asking the models, 'What would you pay for a suit like this?' And that's how we came up with some of the prices. She was so wonderful, I was in the clouds listening to her."

The metallic suit was the hit of the show and upset the market like a tidal wave. It was such a sensation that she had to turn down three out of every four buyers. It was the feature of *Apparel Week*. Pictures of beautiful models wearing the suits appeared in newspapers all over the country, and trade magazines featured it. Rita Hayworth's studio bought one for her, and Rose Marie Reid was instantly famous.

Notes

1. *Vancouver Sun*, 28 November 1938.
2. Jack and Nina Kessler, typed manuscript of interview, n.d. All subsequent comments by Jack and Nina Kessler are from this source unless otherwise noted.
3. *This Week*, September 1956, pp. 8-10.
4. Marjorie Griswald Deposition, 9 September 1955, Docket No. 51225.
5. Ibid.

Glamorous Rita Hayworth in one of Rose Marie's gold metalic swimsuits

While Rose Marie and models watch, Jack Kessler turned the first spadeful of dirt on the $500,000 plant. Rose Marie held the gold swimsuit to be buried on the spot and unearthed in the year 2000.

CHAPTER 7

Rose Marie Reid—Vancouver and California

By 1956, the Rose Marie Reid company had grown from its original 40 sewing machines, a single cutting table, 60 employees, and a staff of three to 1,200 employees, including some 600 sewing machine operators. The five regional offices—Los Angeles, New York City, Chicago, Miami, and Dallas—were staffed by 26 salesmen and five regional directors to service the company's 4500 accounts.[1]

This fantastic growth was due not only to Rose Marie's great gift as a designer, but to her skill as a promoter. "Nobody could promote like her," said Jack Kessler. Of Rose Marie's energy and drive, Jack Kessler said, "Sometimes you move so fast, you don't have time to be scared. . . . That's the way she kept you."

One Saturday, Rose Marie called Jack from Newark, New York, and told him that a man from Banbergers wanted to buy some suits. "Now, Jack, don't go for less than five hundred to a thousand suits," she said. "Just tell him you've got the suits and you're positively going to send them."

"But, Rose Marie, I don't know the man!" pleaded Jack.

"It doesn't matter, just introduce yourself," she replied confidently. He called and told the potential buyer he was sending a thousand suits.

The buyer said, " A thousand suits?"

"He ended up buying and selling every one of them," said Jack.

The first year they had planned to gross $500,000. They exceeded their goal, especially with the help of the metallic fabric. But, ironically, even with these projections, their accountant, a man named Anderson, told Kessler he'd need $75,000 more if they were to stay afloat for the next year.

Feeling enormously pressured, Jack and Nina Kessler charged that their original agreement had called for them only to provide $25,000, not $50,000. Rose Marie was to supply another $25,000 plus her designs and work.

As Rose Marie and the Kesslers sought a legal agreement, lawyers representing each side presented a full history of the verbal agreements before the judge, who decided in favor of Rose Marie. It was not logical, he said, to assume that in addition to the Kesslers' $25,000, Rose Marie was expected to put in $25,000 and also contribute her designs, her work, and the goodwill of her Canadian company on a gratis basis.

As Nina Kessler recounted later, the lawyers and the judge began working out the details of an equitable settlement, while she and Jack sat across the room from Rose Marie. The two parties barely spoke to each other. Said Nina: "To show you how she really was about this whole thing, I was sitting with Jack and our lawyer, she was sitting on the other couch, [while] they were working out the deal. As soon as the deal was signed—that fast!—she came over and started talking and telling us new ideas and giving instructions, as though nothing had ever happened."

Nina also described Rose Marie's ability to take a nap almost on her feet. Rose Marie taught the Kesslers and other employees how to nap this way as well. Rose Marie would often nap in the taxi on her way to an appointment. "Wake me when we get there," she'd say. She would then lay her head back and be instantly out.

George Sobel, one of the company managers, once asked her, "How can you do that?"

"It's simple," she said, "you just tell yourself you're ready to take a nap and then you get on the floor." She would put everybody on the floor with her.

"We looked like a jig-saw puzzle," said Nina Kessler. "Rose

Marie would then say, 'Now close your eyes and go to sleep.' And she could do it on command."

Many tried to entice Rose Marie to leave the new California concern and apply her talents toward their businesses. Rose Marie told Marion about a Mississippi knitting company that offered to double her present salary. The company, which was making 125,000 dozen suits before the war, said, "It's too big for you to answer immediately, but we consider it worth it. We know all about you. Now you learn about us. Then let us know!" Said Rose Marie to Marion, "I realized how sick it will make the Kesslers, and how terrifying business can be, and how uncertain even the best can be. When I had an offer last year, [the Kesslers] were sick, and I salved the hurt by saying, 'Don't you hope I get at least one offer a year to design for someone else?,' and they felt better. But, Marion, [the offer is] fabulous! They said [the salary] could be $100,000 the first year and on up to any volume—they have the money to make it as big a company as I wish. I would love to tell Lou Tabak, who was afraid to go into this business when Jack K. wanted him to. How blessed I am!"[2]

Plant construction of the new Rose Marie Reid factory had begun in 1950. Rose Marie Reid, Nina, and Jack Kessler pressed their handprints into the newly finished cement sidewalk and buried a time capsule containing one of the gold metallic suits that had made her famous. The capsule was to be opened in the year 2000.

In 1951, the Rose Marie Reid company moved into its new quarters on Century Boulevard, near the Los Angeles International Airport. Situated on a three and one-half acre site, the plant held 65,000 square feet of operating space. Future additions increased its size to 125,000 square feet covering nearly eight acres. An auxiliary factory site in downtown Los Angeles held an additional 13,000 square feet.[3]

The sewing floor of the plant was the size of a football field. The employees' cafeteria faced the lovely swimming pool where all of Rose Marie Reid's creations were thoroughly tested. The plant was designed to fit into a $15-million industrial development complex, which Nina Kessler's father, Moses Iflin, had helped design. The plant had an attractive and utilitarian team concept. Working

*Ribbon cutting ceremony for the opening of the new
Rose Marie Reid factory in Canada.*

conditions were excellent, and the smooth work flow was said to be a "marvel" for the age.

"The flow of work starts at the factory receiving dock, which faces Glasgow Avenue," reported the *California Apparel News*. "Receiving is equipped to store a reserve of approximately 300,000 yards of material (fabrics). From there work passes directly into the 38,000 square foot cutting room, on into the sewing room, down the lines, into pressing, finishing, final inspection and shipping, all in one continuous line of operation."[4]

At the same time Rose Marie was busy building her California company, she was still running her factory in Vancouver. In 1947, just four years before opening the Los Angeles factory, she built a new factory in Vancouver. Unfortunately, the new building would never see much of Rose Marie's on-the-job genius. The grand opening was a formal affair with full press coverage and honored by the attendance of many Canadian dignitaries. The children—Bruce, 11, Sharon, 9, and Carole, 7—were present to cut the ribbon to open the doors of the larger and more modern facility.

This expansion was of great concern to Rose Marie. She was anxious about the additional overhead and the maintenance costs of the spacious building. Too much of the working capital had been drained from the company; so in order to keep the Canadian firm afloat, she negotiated a loan from the Bank of Nova Scotia for $100,000, secured by one Billy Jardine. Unfortunately, Jardine died in 1951 and his heirs called the note, leaving the Canadian company in an untenable cash position.

To develop her California operation, Rose Marie had left her Canadian company in the capable hands of H. H. ("Bob") Marcou. A series of letters saved from Rose Marie's relationship with Marcou reveal the growth and subsequent decline of the Canadian company. In 1949 he sent her a draft on the Bank of Toronto for 9,185.94 Canadian dollars (no doubt her 1949 profits), with this note appended: "I thought this might make an acceptable Christmas gift."[5]

As her California company took more and more of her time, Marcou was growing worried, wrote Rose Marie to Marion, "how to hold the beautiful profit he has made in swimsuits this year and I have no Fall line (housecoats, etc.) for him, and he is hunting savagely on his own. He is justly put out that I cannot help. I have no time. Yet designing is my job in the firm. He has assumed every other responsibility."[6]

Upon the death of Jardine, who had secured the money to sustain the Canadian company, Rose Marie was forced to approach the Kesslers and convince them that it would be in their best interest to buy the worldwide rights to the name, "Rose Marie Reid." Kessler agreed, and arranged for loans from two banks, one in Seattle and the other in Toronto. The Canadian company was barely hanging on, and Marcou tried desperately to keep it alive. He went to great lengths to lease Rose Marie's name to other clothiers in Canada, and for a time was successful. Silver and Company, another Canadian clothier, leased the rights for a ten-year period but was apparently unable to continue the arrangement.

Kessler, seeing the precipitous decline in the Canadian business after his purchase, frantically wanted out of the arrangement. Since Rose Marie had essentially asked him to buy the company, she felt obligated to assume the loss. She did this by signing over to him 150 shares of her stock in the California company. At some other time she had sold or traded 100 other shares to Kessler's father-in-law, Moses Iflin. This would have still left Rose Marie with a healthy interest in the California company, except that Kessler had issued himself, unbeknown to Rose Marie, an additional 500 shares of stock, thus diluting her interest to nearly ten percent. This move later became the subject of legal debate.

Rose Marie knew that her Canadian company was in decline and that her time and efforts had to be with the California company. But she remained concerned about the people she had left behind in Canada, and her correspondence reflects this. In one letter she expresses her interest in an employee named Vince, who apparently had some very personal problems. He was one of their most dedicated employees and had to spend a lot of time on the road. This made his wife, "a nervous little thing," quite edgy to have him out of her sight. Rose Marie proposed that Bob allow Vince's wife to accompany him on a working vacation.

As late as 27 March 1951, Bob Marcou wrote Rose Marie on Rose Marie Reid, Inc., letterhead. "I might as well accept the fact you've given up Canada," he said. Said Rose Marie to Marion, "Mr. Marcou was [in California] for a few days, and I was sad when he left for he was beginning to get a complex about the smallness of the Canadian business and lack of opportunities there, when he could come to the U.S. and do what several Canadians have done—succeed spectacularly. Also, there was so much going on around me, he went to fabric places and saw how they treat me as though my every word was something they could make money out of. . . . I told him to sell the factory and move here. He has such superior ability, he could get a highly paid job so fast. . . . That space at the top is so horribly empty! We need so many top ability men. Not to have to develop them, but ready made. If we could get 10-20 we would be so much better off. It breaks my heart that my brothers cannot be part of it."

In this letter Rose Marie's plea to her sister is a reminder of their close relationship: "Marion, I cannot stand it if you do not come this summer. My personal life is little enough, and we must not grow apart. That wonderful nearness and love of you had made my whole life so full and made up for so much else. I do hope my two girls will have it. Nothing will ever effect [sic] them if they have."[7]

On 10 October 1952 Marcou sent letters to all creditors that "Rose Marie Reid, Inc.," of Canada was closing its doors. Six months later he wrote to Kessler and Rose Marie in California, "I did not do my career any good by sticking with the ship." He had a job offer in Toronto at $10,000 a year with stock in the company. It is interesting to note that Rose Marie was pleased that his new home would be within "easy walking distance of the [Mormon] Church."[7] Always a missionary for her beliefs, Rose Marie wanted Bob near the mission president in Toronto so he could get some good gospel conversation, for she had carried on a dialogue about the Church with him for many years, and she was hopeful that someday he would be baptized.

Never one to look back, Rose Marie wrote to Marion of her burgeoning business in California. "My new designs look exciting. . . . It looks like a . . . no, not a gold mine, but a diamond mine."[8] Now it was time to bring her children to California.

Notes

1. "America's Miracle, Free Enterprise in Action in Southern California: The Little Swimsuit Has Become Big Business," *Los Angeles Times*, 8 May 1956, Part I-12.
2. Letter to Marion Heilner, n.d.
3. "America's Miracle," *Los Angeles Times*.
4. *California Apparel News*, 7 September 1951.
5. H. H. "Bob" Marcou, letter to Rose Marie Reid, 22 December 1949.
6. Rose Marie Reid, letter to Marion Heilner, 8 June 1951.
7. Rose Marie Reid, letter to Marion Heilner, 11 June 1953.
8. Rose Marie Reid, letter to Marion Heilner, n.d.

Rose Marie traveled between Canada and the United States, purchasing fabrics and marketing her fashions to department stores in both countries. Here she receives an award from United Airlines for the many miles flown.

CHAPTER 8

Long-Distance Mother

It took Rose Marie's California company three years to begin making substantial enough profits for Rose Marie to afford a home. Canadian postwar restrictions permitted only $750 per year to be taken out of the country by any individual, so it was impossible to use money from the Canadian business to relocate the family. It was an exhausting process for Rose Marie to get her children into the United States. Immigration obstacles, such as permanent visas, were lengthy and difficult.

Meanwhile, the children were anxious to join their mother in California. They had been eagerly waiting to hear that she had a home for them, and they would be living where the sun always shines and the palm trees grow tall. It was like a fairy tale to them. Too young to realize the complications connected with their relocation, they were excited at the prospect of the new adventure.

While Rose Marie was setting up her business in California, her children had not been unhappy living in Canada. Marie watched over them during the school year; the children also had a nanny. Whenever Rose Marie returned from her travels, she always brought a present for Bruce and story book dolls for Sharon and Carole. "We had such a collection," said Sharon.

The children lived comfortably in the home that Rose Marie had fixed up for them. She had papered every wall and hooked every rug and made every drape. She had reupholstered an old sofa, having first taken it entirely apart. Someone had thrown it away, and she took wooden crates and reinforced and rewired it entirely. She had also replaced all the old springs. She had even built a room in the basement for Bruce, nailing every board into place herself. Sharon saw the house all torn apart, and she saw it all put back together, and it was "lovely."

When Rose Marie still had the Vancouver factory, the children would take the street car that stopped right near their house. All of the street car drivers knew the Reid children and would let them out right in front of the factory in downtown Vancouver. At night the street car drivers would take the children to the corner nearest their home, and wait until they got to their front door.

"We grew up with the smell of bolts of fabric and sewing machines," said Sharon. The workers at the factory loved the children, and they held parties and made doll clothes for them. "One year for Christmas we got trunks with a doll and a whole wardrobe for the dolls." Carole and Sharon always got identical gifts and were always dressed exactly alike. "Every dress we ever wore and every toy we ever received were always two exactly alike." Carole finally rebelled, saying she was not a twin and she didn't want to be treated like twins.

At times Rose Marie would create jobs at the factory so the children would learn to work. Sharon and Carole both had real jobs there. They cut out totem poles to sew on the suits. "Mother gave us a lecture the first day. 'When you're the boss's child, you have to be there earlier than anyone else, you have to wait till everyone else has gone to lunch before you can go. You also must be the first ones back from lunch, and you're always the last to stop work in the evening.'" She took them to the back room and told them exactly how the business worked.

Sharon always remembered an experience she had as a young girl that portrayed the type of honesty inherent in Rose Marie. "I was working with her at the factory. There were nearly one thousand seamstresses, and the company had thousands of spools of thread in every color. The sewers worked so quickly that they always kept their spool full and would discard their nearly empty spools before the thread was completely gone. The spools would be sorted and the thread rewound onto full spools.

"One day I went to the bins full of the partially empty thread and chose some of the colors I needed for sewing at home. I certainly reasoned that it was such a little bit compared to the vast amount used on a daily basis, and the company belonged to us anyway. We were driving home together when Mother saw the thread in my bag. She stopped the car and said to me that the thread was not hers, that it belonged to the company, and that we could not take it just because it was there. We turned around during the rush hour traffic to return the nearly empty spools of thread."

Her entire life Rose Marie would never lock her car or her house. She simply felt that most people were honest. Said Sharon, "With Mother there was no degree attached to honesty, no rationalizing or compromising, and she simply assumed that all people felt the same way."

Because Rose Marie was traveling and not able to follow through with the children's studies, she enrolled them in a private school in Canada. The girls went to York House, and Bruce went to a boarding school and came home on weekends. He hated it. For years Rose Marie regretted sending him there. The schools were very expensive. Because of postwar food rationing, all of the school children had to contribute their ration coupons. The staff pooled these coupons and thereby improved the quality of food for the school. The children ate their main midday meals there. They wore uniforms and were tutored by very rigid, but very capable, instructors.

On occasion, when one of the children was assigned a talk for church or school while Rose Marie was in California or traveling, they would write out their talk and mail it to her. She would read it carefully, making improvements and telling them where to use less or more voice inflection, where to pause, and where to really arouse the audience. Often she'd suggest a better ending or an anecdote, and always she would ask them to memorize the talk completely. When that was done, they'd sometimes tape record it and send it off to her; sometimes they would rehearse it for her over the phone.

She read every term paper and listened to every song they sang. "She was interested in every facet of our lives," said Carole. "Once I drew a picture of what I wanted my prom dress to be. She made it and had her models sew on sequins."

It didn't take long for the children to realize their mother was famous—in fact, she became somewhat of a fairy princess. Sometimes she would come to the children's school. "It always caused such a stir when she came because she was so beautiful. She was like a movie star," Carole recalled. Their classmates, who were children of the rich, were in awe of her, and Rose Marie's children enjoyed the attention. Among these classmates were the Grahams, who entertained the king and queen of England, and the Graxis children, whose father was a well-known Greek shipping magnate in Canada. Sharon remembered going to a birthday party where ice cream was served. "[It] was so hard to get after the war, but it was a very wealthy family and they picked us up in a limousine."

Rose Marie made many sacrifices for the children's education; certainly her income did not come close to that of the other children's parents. In fact, this was the period when money was very scarce. "I remember wearing the same red-and-white stripe knit sweater to church again and again. Each year mother would just knit another stripe to make it longer. I hated that sweater because the white stripe was of angora, and it made my nose itch," remembered Carole. But to provide for their education and training, Rose Marie would have sacrificed all.

Rose Marie herself was an accomplished pianist, so she exposed her three children to wonderful music. She would sit with them at the piano and play the classics, and they would plead for her to play the famous Funeral March and tell them the story of a little boy who had died. "As she would tell the story, she would get tears in her eyes. We loved to have her do it, but we'd all end up in tears," said Sharon.

Rose Marie immersed the children in the culture of music, books, people, and especially religion. Carole remembered "sitting through the *Messiah* several times, thinking these were the longest nights of my life. . . . But, of course, now I love every minute of it." When the children joined their mother in their new home in California on Bundy Drive, one of their neighbors was Gregor Pedagorsky, the world-renowned cellist of the Los Angeles Philharmonic Orchestra. He showed great patience with the children, their noise, parties, and friends. He also tolerated Bruce's BB gun. "He was always gracious and wonderful to us," said Sharon.

The children always had lessons of some kind—ballet, elocution, or ice skating. Every weekend they would skate, and several times they participated in ice shows. Sharon was once featured in the *Vancouver Sun* newspaper for her performance.

Jack Reid had taught the children to be excellent swimmers. "We never just jumped off the diving board, we always had to dive off, and we always had to dive beautifully," said Sharon. During the beginning years of the company, Rose Marie designed swimsuits for children, using her own children as models. "Sometimes it was boring and long having pictures taken all the time," said Carole. With the move to Los Angeles, children's suits were dropped from production.

The children knew that their mother valued their opinions even when they were very young. "She never treated us like children," said Sharon. "We often sat in on business discussions, and she would always ask our opinions. From the time we were six or seven, we felt a part of her business from our choice of fabrics and our ideas for designs. We would buy fabric with her, and she would let us help her choose. If the sales people laughed at us or tried to send us out with a candy bar, she would let them know that we were capable of making decisions. Sometimes I think she designed a swimsuit just to show us that we were important to her."

Every Easter, the family traveled to Baker, Oregon, to visit their Aunt Marion and Uncle Sanford. "It was the highlight of our lives to travel to see our Boise and Baker cousins," said Sharon. The only problem the children had with these visits was that during the whole trip Rose Marie would talk to them about religion. "We sang hymns and she would tell us stories from the scriptures and teach us the doctrines of the Church. Sometimes I would plead with her," said Carole, "Please, don't talk religion anymore!" That never stopped Rose Marie, however; she felt that the area of her children's training that she could not leave to someone else was the truths they needed to know about the gospel, and she never missed an opportunity to teach them.

"I thought sometimes I never wanted to hear another Joseph Smith story, but I know now she taught me to love him and his testimony. He restored the truth, and I'm so thankful she schooled us well," said Carole. The children anticipated the trip to Baker each year with so much excitement that when they finally arrived, their visit would always go by too quickly. As they sadly prepared to return home, Rose Marie would depart and lovingly say to Marion, "I'll see you next Easter, and that will just be the day after tomorrow."

Some of the most tender moments for the children were spent with their Grandma Yancey. She wore her white braided hair on top of her head, and the children would sit on her lap in the kitchen rocking chair as she would tell them stories. Night after night, Marie put them to bed with stories of their mother, constantly reminding them of her love for them.

Where her children were concerned, Rose Marie had a sixth sense. She always seemed to know when something was wrong. Once they were playing dolls with a neighbor friend, and they put a dog into the carriage and dressed him like a baby. He became so irritated that he jumped at Sharon and nearly bit off her nose. While Marie was cleaning up the blood, Rose Marie called from New York and asked what was wrong. "She knew something was wrong," said Sharon.

Rose Marie told one *Los Angeles Times* reporter, "I'm a long-distance mother right now, but even my mother says I'm a good mother."[1] Bruce often commented that he was raised by telephone.

Carole retains a letter from her mother which is signed, "Your mother—and what a joy that title gives me!"[2] Truly, the greatest gift that Rose Marie bestowed upon her children was her tremendous love for them. She truly understood the infinite worth of her children, and they were always secure in that knowledge.

When Rose Marie went house-hunting, she was strongly tempted by a house in Glendale in the Flintridge District. It had been built twenty years earlier for the famous actor Victor McLaughlin. She learned that several other Mormon families lived in the area, and she met the stake president, Nephi Anderson, who told her he was dividing the Glendale Ward and making a new La Canada Ward.

Rose Marie invited him to build the new church "in the lemon grove back of the house," when she bought it. He met with the zoning commission and found that it would be possible to build a church in the area. However, the deal fell through and Rose Marie wasn't able to buy the house after all.

Not long after that, she pulled into the driveway of a beautiful house at 334 South Bundy Drive in Brentwood. She knew immediately that *this* was to be her home. She was so excited when she saw it that the owners immediately took it off the market and raised the price. Nevertheless, she still bought it. Six miles from the Santa Monica beaches, the house was also very close to the site upon which the Mormon temple was later built in Los Angeles. At that time the smog had not reached that far west, and the sky was crisp and blue.

"The home spoke to me, and I knew it was right," said Rose Marie. It was near to her brother Hugh and his family so they could watch out for the children and "be family with them." Rose Marie always called the home and property her "celestial kingdom" here on earth.

The home was originally built by a famous movie producer, Woody Van Dyke, who came from Germany during the 1920s. During the 1930s he was one of the big powers in Hollywood. Dixie Hussey, one of Rose Marie's neighbors, had watched the mansion being built and was a friend of the Van Dyke family. In those years Brentwood was a rural area, and it was considered a long distance to Hollywood. The Husseys recalled that their dogs chased rabbits, and they could see almost to the ocean. There was also a fully equipped bomb shelter and stables and corrals for horses.

In June of 1949, Rose Marie was thrilled when at long last she was joined in California by her three children: Bruce, Sharon, and Carole.

Notes

1. Fay Hammond, "Miss Reid Suits Swimmer Best, " *Los Angeles Times*, 18 December 1955, Part III-B, C.
2. Letter from Rose Marie Reid to Carole Reid Burr, n.d. (Park Lane Hotel, New York City).

The Rose Marie Reid estate in Brentwood, California

CHAPTER 9

A New Home

Bruce, Sharon, and Carole Reid arrived in Los Angeles on a Greyhound bus accompanied by one of their Canadian nannies, Aunt Lil. Concerned that Jack would prevent the children from leaving Vancouver, Rose Marie had instructed Lil not to tell anyone when she and the children were leaving. However, out of some sense of loyalty to Jack, Aunt Lil notified him of their departure just before they left Vancouver.

"This cost Mother a great deal of money, but we were not sure why," said Sharon. When they arrived in Los Angeles, Rose Marie fired Lil on the spot. Sharon had never seen her mother as angry and hurt as she was at that moment.

The children arrived in California, recalled Sharon, wearing "underpants made from flour sacks and walking into a Brentwood estate." Rose Marie picked them up at the bus depot in a beautiful new Cadillac.

When they drove up to the property, the gates were closed, so they got out of the car, opened the gate, and started up the driveway. They were stunned by what appeared to them to be a "fairyland or movie set." Sharon said, "I saw the garage and thought that was the house, for it was so gorgeous, and then when I looked off to the side and there was the house, I about died." The children were nearly speechless at the long driveway lined with the anticipated palm trees, the swimming pool, orange trees, and what seemed like acres of lawn.

"The mansion had no furniture," said Carole. "We just camped and got lost inside—so many hallways, bathrooms, and fireplaces. There was a separate laundry house and one room that looked like the inside of a ship. It was a wet bar, something we knew very little of, but we loved the porthole windows and the glass aquarium with rare tropical fish. We fed the fish constantly, and we felt so sad when they all died in a few weeks," said Carole. She wanted to tell all her friends back in Vancouver how her dreams had come true. The home, the citrus trees, the flowers and beaches—all were so beautiful in California.

Everyone thought Sharon was homesick because she would go into her room alone and take out things from a box she had brought with her from Canada. She was always writing things in her little book, and she wanted someone to read to her continually from *Mr. Popper's Penguins*, her favorite children's book. But Sharon was not lonely, she was entranced. She would go into the large sewing room and drape fabric over the mannequin, pretending she was a famous designer. "It was just my heaven. . . . I couldn't believe it all," said Sharon.

That whole first day, Rose Marie played in the pool with the children. She also knocked on the doors of the neighbors' houses and asked if they had children the same ages as hers. The Husseys had three children close to the ages of Rose Marie's children, and for years the two families were good friends. Mrs. Hussey described the sight of "Rose Marie going out in her big Cadillac, swinging out early in the morning. . . . Pretty soon over would come Carole. I would check her over and make sure she was presentable for school. Sometimes I would tie a shoe or fix a hem. It was great fun for me because it made me sort of belong to another couple of people. I enjoyed them all very much." The Hussey family often swam with Rose Marie's children in the pool.[1]

Rose Marie opened the house to clubs, civic groups, and wards and stakes in the Church. The home soon became the center of activity for the Church in the area. People came from all over the country and stayed with her. "It got to be so much in demand that I wouldn't know who I was waking up to in the morning," said

Carole. The kitchen was constantly full of people fixing food. They used the pool, held fashion shows, and had luncheons; special friends and family would stay overnight. Jan Warner, Rose Marie's personal secretary and a close friend of the family, coordinated all scheduling for the mansion.

Rose Marie hired an African-American housekeeper and groundskeeper. This was the children's first exposure to African-Americans. "At first we were very curious, but soon they were our friends. I remember asking our first housekeeper how she knew if she had a sun tan," said Carole. Grandmother Yancey came to live there, and so did her sister, Florence Sherk. Aunt Florence was notorious for her difficult temperament, but she was greatly needed. She managed the house, did the shopping, and kept everyone working. It was very hard to keep hired help because Florence was so difficult. Finally, Josephine Grassi, another African-American housekeeper, joined the staff; she and Aunt Florence became good friends. However, although Josephine could clean, her cooking was awful.

Jan Warner said, "When Rose Marie had company for dinner, it wasn't 'What shall we serve?' It was, 'Josephine, pick up the chicken.'"[2] To Marion, Rose Marie wrote, "Frozen foods are heaven. We had such flawless spinach and two kinds of berry pie. It was so nice not to have to worry if the pie would be good."[3]

Rose Marie's mother found the new home and beautiful surroundings to be a great worry. It was hard for her to deal with the new affluence, and she told her son Hugh that her two worries were "him and Rose Marie's house." To calm her fears, Rose Marie teased her mother, saying that she hadn't actually bought the house, just the swimming pool. "They threw the house in and I couldn't help it if it had a couple more rooms than I really needed."[4] Toying with her mother, Rose Marie said playfully, "I couldn't just say I'll take all but these two rooms."

Privately, however, Marie was relieved that Rose Marie was in such pleasant surroundings. She told Marion, "Did you know Gary Cooper, Joan Crawford, Shirley Temple, and several more stars live right near us?" With some remorse she admitted, "But there are times I want my little home in Boise. I feel like Papa is near when I'm there."[5]

Hugh assured Marie that the house was a fantastic deal and that Rose Marie could double her money by reselling it "right today or [in] ten years." The worth of the property in 1992 was over eight million dollars.

Rose Marie kept four Cadillacs. Each year she would rotate the last one and give it to her brother Don, who was struggling financially. When relatives and friends came to town, they always had access to one of her cars.

Luther Hussey, one of Bruce's friends, said, "I felt like the strangest person in the world picking up firewood at different places for your mother in the back of Fleetwood Cadillacs! I think those were the most expensive pickup trucks that had ever been designed. Of course, I disliked the job of driving those gorgeous cars around on errands," continued Luther, tongue in cheek, "but we were able to do it—groceries and all the other things she would have us do."[6]

According to Jan Warner, "This little community of permanent residents consisted of Rose Marie and her children . . . , Marie Yancey and her sister, Florence Sherk." Marie and Florence often drove one of the Cadillacs to Knotts Berry Farm for dinner. Josephine, and Florence often "disappeared and went for rides in the Cadillacs." The two women got along well. "'Aunt' Florence needed Josephine," said Jan. Josephine was "somebody she was over, and this was important to her."

Rose Marie's mornings began at 5:00 a.m. (she seldom went to bed before 1:00 a.m.). After she was awake, her Aunt Florence, who was a trained masseuse, would give her a morning massage. This would prepare Rose Marie for a strenuous day of work. Rose Marie always claimed that Aunt Florence had magic fingers. She could massage away hours of tension and stress.

On many mornings, when Florence heard Rose Marie coming down to the breakfast table, she would dash to the sink and empty her coffee cup. The Mormon code of health forbids drinking coffee, and Florence didn't want Rose Marie to know that she indulged in the forbidden drink. One day when Jan was out shopping in Brentwood, she came upon Florence sitting at a sidewalk cafe drinking her coffee and having a doughnut. Jan retraced her steps quickly so as not to offend Florence. Everyone knew Florence drank coffee, and it seemed almost a game, pretending not to know. But Rose Marie insisted that everyone preserve Florence's dignity and not embarrass her.

"Looking back," said Sharon, "we all realize that not only did Aunt Florence need us, but we needed her." She drove the children to all of their school functions. "I know we drove her crazy and often we felt the same about her, but she was always willing to help us any time of the day or night," said Carole.

The yard was like a beautiful park. Groups often used it for fund-raising activities, and many friends had wedding receptions there. One Saturday morning, Jan woke up early and heard someone swimming in the pool. Rose Marie rarely swam, so Jan knew it wasn't her. Very soon a neighbor phoned, complaining about the early morning swimming. Jan put on her robe walked out to the pool and found a perfect stranger swimming. Jan motioned for her to get out of the pool and asked who she was. The strange woman, she learned, had recently moved into the neighborhood. "I heard that the pool was available to anyone," she said.

Summers were always filled with visitors and relatives. Some would come the whole summer and some for short visits. When visitors came, Rose Marie went out of her way to take them to the newly built temple and make certain they were entertained. Cleon and Jewel Skousen, and their nine children, were eleven such visitors. Jewel said of the wonderful hospitality, "It was like having a second home in Los Angeles." Rose Marie arranged gatherings for Cleon, who was a well-known Mormon scholar and historian, to speak, and she invited many to her home to meet his family.

Dixie Hussey told Carole, "Your mother was always gracious whenever she saw us. She was a busy little woman and worked awfully hard. I don't know how she did it at all. She once took me down to the Rose Marie Reid factory, and I was overwhelmed with her ability and how everybody was so polite to her; of course, she was the leading lady." Rose Marie made suits for the Hussey family because some styles weren't available in the needed sizes. Said Dixie, "We thought we were about the hottest thing since sliced bread because we had our own custom-designed bathing suits. . . . I always had Rose Marie Reid bathing suits, which were the best bathing suits one ever had."[7]

Around the house Rose Marie was a "list maker." She made lists for everyone—visitors, relatives, children, housekeepers. Hundreds

Rose Marie's bedroom

of concerns were always going through her head simultaneously. Sometimes she was so tired that in the middle of making a list she fell asleep, her writing slurring down to an unintelligible squiggle. When this happened, she would wake with a start and continue the list. She wrote lists about designing problems, family, church, quotes from famous people, and scriptures. "I'm certain she fell asleep while writing many of the notes because if her body slowed down enough to write a letter, she would get sleepy. I'm sure it felt, 'this is my chance' and it would take a nap," said Sharon. One note reveals Rose Marie's interest in the Jewish people: "Hebraic history has certain identifying Hebraisms—God's dealings with the Chosen ppl." Another cites the saying, "She must not be taken for granted—yet she must have the security of being taken for granted." Another note to the children reads, "Clean your rooms, say your prayers!"

Rose Marie wrote long, long lists to her gardener. She was a part of every decision about the rose beds, the shrubbery, and the lawns. "Will the roses by the pool . . . ever grow, or should we plant new climbing red roses there?" she wrote to the gardener. Patiently the man replied point by point to her seven-page inquiry about the smallest details. "Yes, they will, as long as they are fertilized and watered well." "Red leaves are characteristic of the plant. However, fertilizing three times annually plus H_2O will keep it much greener." "Weeding is the only way to keep geraniums free from weeds." And so it went, question after question, until all of her concerns for that day were answered.

Living as she did in the world of high fashion, Rose Marie felt it was vital that she be perceived as young and progressive. To her, a youthful image gave her authority in matters of fashion and charm and helped her to fill the needs of both the young and the old. A young and attractive appearance gave her a necessary credibility. When Fay Hammond of the *Los Angeles Times* interviewed her for her award as "Woman of the Year," Hammond thought she was about thirty. Actually, she was just a few months away from her fiftieth birthday.[8]

One time she wrote to Marion and told her that if Marion didn't start fibbing about her age, Rose Marie was going to become her younger sister, not her older sister. She always smudged her birthdate on her driver's license and never admitted to being any older than thirty-two.

Whenever she got a new passport, she would drop fingernail polish over her birth year and then peel it off. Frustrated, passport agents always stopped her, and she'd smile and say, "Oh, I must have spilled something on it." One time before leaving the country for an international tour, she said to Carole, "Every bellboy in Europe handles your passport. They needn't all know my age." Even now, there is no birthdate on her gravestone.

One of Rose Marie's beauty secrets was her "frowning paper." She believed that if she taped brown sticky paper to her face where wrinkles were likely to appear, she could stop them from coming. She always wore a V-shaped paper on her forehead while sleeping or working about the house, while designing, and even while driving. She hated wrinkles, and she hated anyone to know her true age.

Rose Marie always recommended to the family and friends that they wear "frowning paper." The only one who consistently took her advice was her personal secretary, Jan, and today Jan has no wrinkles. "We thought all mothers had frowning paper," said Rose Marie's daughter Carole.

At Rose Marie's death in 1978, Carole "stood at her casket, looking down into her beautiful unwrinkled face, and in my mind I said to her, 'Well, Mother, those frowning papers worked.'"

Notes

1. Dixie Hussey, interview, 27 July 1988.
2. Jan Warner, interview, n.d. All subsequent comments from Jan Warner are taken from this source.
3. Letter, Rose Marie Reid to Marion Heilner, n.d.
4. Letter, Rose Marie Reid to Marion Heilner, n.d.
5. Marion Heilner, interview.
6. Luther Hussey, interview, 27 July 1988. All subsequent comments from Luther Hussey are taken from this source.
7. Dixie Hussey, interview.
8. Hammond, "Miss Reid Suits Swimmer Best," *Los Angeles Times.*

*Rose Marie held firmly to the philosophy that "a woman should
feel as lovely in a swimsuit as she does in an evening gown."*

CHAPTER 10

The Little Swimsuit Is Big Business

Rose Marie was only three years old when Jantzen, one of her biggest competitors, began manufacturing swimsuits. Such a head start should have been an insurmountable barrier, but as Rose Marie entered the marketplace she saw that Jantzen, along with the other manufacturers, were operating from at least two erroneous assumptions—"that all women were created equal and that they were all cast in the image of beauty pageant queens."[1]

With this in mind, Rose Marie began making swimsuits for all women, catering to needs long neglected by the industry giants. She made suits for real figures, addressing special needs of women of all sizes and ages.

In creating her designs, Rose Marie divided the female figure into six geometric areas and created camouflaging devices for each to hide imperfections. For the full figure, she created a "bodice bra with plastic boning and several rows of hooks and eyes that yielded a 'natural divided bustline look.'"[2] For the heavy hipped, she recommended a slimming dress-like suit with vertical stripes to "lead the eye away from the hipline and give the illusion of slimness."[3] To keep the bottom up, she worked out a "smudge a curve, nudge a curve"[4] support system that molded and shaped the figure. And her

The "magic length" swimsuit

tummy control panels held smoothly any extra inches in the tummy area. She created a stay-down leg on the panty, made possible by a crotch of novel design. For the tall, long-bodied figure, she designed the "magic length" that had several inches of material that could be stretched down as far as necessary without distorting the design.

Women who had never been able to buy bathing suits found that they could now buy a suit that would camouflage their figure faults. They could wear a Rose Marie Reid suit with perfect ease and comfort, knowing that they looked their best. Furthermore, Rose Marie was adamant about "never designing an immodest bathing suit." Rose Marie believed that most women really wanted to be modestly covered, and they wanted self-perceived defects hidden. Marjorie Griswald made this statement in her personal correspondence with Rose Marie: "What customers do know is that your suits do something for them no other suits can do, and when they need a new suit, they will always be back for one of yours. And you will always have lots of good ones."[5]

This approach capsized the industry and forced her competition, the "big four" (Jantzen, Catalina, Cole, and Mabs), to copy her designs. In another letter, Marjorie wrote, "You certainly are right about the many copies of principles. They are all over the market, every time I see a bathing suit picture it reminds me of something you had done before. However, it is a nice compliment, though infuriating. The problem it poses for you though is a rough one, for you have to come up with the new ideas, then sweat, blood and tears that they can follow."[6] For the rest of her career, Rose Marie would be plagued by people stealing her designs. Said one of Rose Marie's "big four" competitors: "We copied all of her suits; so did the other three concerns. I mean 100 percent. The companies that didn't are now out of business."[7]

During one of her numerous flights, Rose Marie wrote to Marion, " I'm so astonished because other people have copied them so closely that I cannot tell the difference in store stock sometimes. The stewardess just said to me, 'Oh I have your suits and my boyfriend sells your fabrics (Bates). He was at a Cole show last week and they said, "The suit they call 'Rose Marie' they should call Rose 'Marie Reid' for we stole it from her.'"[8]

By 1948, local papers across America featured pictures of Rose Marie, her models, and her swimsuits. Jane Allen of the *Oregonian* wrote: "Mrs. Reid designs suits that look as perishable and as pretty as a strawberry ice cream soda but shed water like a duck, move with every muscle but prove as adjustable to that motion as one's own skin."[9] Rose Marie was still using most of her earlier patented control devices, but had added some new features. The built-in wired bra was improved, and elastic banding helped streamline figures. Brief skirt sections made even "big girls" feel comfortable. Straps that adjusted for bosom support, shirrings that pushed at waistlines that were out of tune, and paneling to redistribute body padding that was too generous in the wrong places all contributed to the Rose Marie Reid look.

Her fabrics were revolutionary. She used whites with thin gold metallic strips, white-and-gold diamond-patterned mattelasse, all-gold mattelasse, and candy-pink and silver stripes that looked as though they'd been cut from ballroom gown patterns but were as durable and water resistant as "a mermaid's scales."[10] She loved pastels and dark colors, which seemed to have the best characteristics for hiding defects. Her creations were pictured on television newsreels and magazine covers. Terry Hatley and Lee Gore, nationally known models, paraded her one-piece princess and two-piece all-figure design on the front of *Home* magazine.

In 1950 Rose Marie designed a bra that buttoned out of the suit so it could be worn with strapless summer dresses or evening gowns, and her crisp cottons, which refused to lose their shape or patterns when wet, made her suits strong competitors wherever they showed. Also in 1950 she did "the impossible by making a strapless swim suit with a back so low that it defied all laws of nature (stopping scarcely three inches above the waist)."[11] Still, her featured sales push was that she had become "dear to the hearts of the larger ladies, for she has done MUCH to make them pretty in bathing suits."[12]

The fifties were Rose Marie's years. *Esquire* featured her lead creation of the 1951 season on Valentine's day with a full-page, multicolor photo—a suit that "clings to sun-tanned torsos like molten gold."[13] Actually it was gold, 24-carat plated onto black lace fabric, and advertised as "the suit of the year." It was sold exclusively by Lord and Taylor as the top of the Rose Marie Reid line, selling for over $100 a suit. But Rose Marie's line also appeared in papers like the Memphis *Commercial Appeal* with suits averaging around $12.00 each. The "Sculptured" line featured the "Sea Sheath" at $12.95 and the "Shirred Sunner" at $17.95. Both became favorite designs of the everyday American woman.

The combined hard work and enthusiasm of the Kesslers and Rose Marie made a product in which the customers had great confidence. As a result of their success, they formed a national sales organization. Not only did their advertising budget include newspaper and magazine advertising, but they spent 50 percent of their budget on point-of-sale promotion. Slowly Rose Marie Reid, Inc., established new merchandising methods. Previously, the swimsuit business had habitually produced one line of suits a year; Rose Marie daringly came out with a small but new line for late summer.

*The heralded Hourglass swimsuit was selected throughout Europe
and the United States as the outstanding design in 1951.*

This late season line did so well that other manufacturers adopted the idea. Midwinter promotions made another line of suits available for the cruise ship and Florida resort seasons. By introducing several new lines, Rose Marie revolutionized the swimwear market, which now became a year-round business.

It was the "Hourglass" design in 1951 that catapulted Rose Marie Reid into the international markets. *Life* magazine chose this suit as the most outstanding and revolutionary suit of the year, and gave it full-page color coverage in their magazine.[14] Ms. Griswald had just been to Paris choosing the "bests" for the year. Upon arriving in New York and seeing the Empire Hourglass, she also chose it as the year's best; consequently, Lord & Taylor featured Rose Marie's suits in a fabulous window display in New York. The windows were called "Jewels of the Sea," and all of Lord and Taylor's windows on

Rose Marie was one of the first designers to add accessories to swimsuits.

Fifth Avenue were devoted to this display for several weeks.

In 1951, the company had risen to an annual gross income of $3,500,000. Edith "Tiennie" Greenberg took over as vice president in charge of merchandise control. She achieved an enviable reputation among buyers throughout the sales areas for her adherence to the quality the "designer had in mind." Harry Cohen was made treasurer, and Kessler appointed his own brother, Henry, as purchasing director. A. H. Eisenberg was the credit manager and export head, and B. R. "Bing" Miller was production manager. They had 700 employees. Within six months they topped well over 1,000.

Writing to Marion on 9 January 1952, Rose Marie said, "Other years I have told you how nice it is to be recognized as an authority. Well, this year everyone big and little is positively kow-towing. I had not realized the impact the hour-glass had had. . . . It's stupendous. Our office is mobbed, every day of the week. People sitting all around the room, and today even buyers on the floor. Sometimes people wait 4 days for an appointment to even get into the door and be part of the mob. Nothing like it in history. One buyer said, 'The rest of the market in N.Y. is so dead, it's a pleasure to come in here and know that somewhere there is activity.'"[15] The same types of crowds were mobbing the Chicago, New Orleans, Miami, and Los Angeles offices. Saks of Miami phoned the Los Angeles plant and said, "Send us 1,000 of anything that you have and 500 more for Palm Beach at once." She pleaded to Marion, "Pray for me to be good again next year. . . . How can I equal it? Not try to top it. Griswald of L&T says they will be very happy to give me windows again."[16]

Rose Marie was so busy she could not travel to New York to see the windows. Marjorie wrote to her: "It is a shame you didn't see the windows, because they were absolutely breathtaking. The two young men who now do them spent more effort than any others except Christmas. And they showed it. We had pictures taken for you, but the windows would certainly have given you great delight to see. Of course sales have been phenomenal in all the stores. We can't seem to have enough on hand, a thousand suits seems inadequate. . . . The results have been wonderful. The windows created tremendous customer and trade comment and Lastex sales have out run cotton in May and June for the first time ever."[17]

The Hourglass appeared in every magazine of note. In *Life* it showed in the same display with a Schiaparelli one-piece, and the difference was so startling that it amazed and dumbfounded readers everywhere. And a Jacques Heim bikini was a positive shame in comparison. The latter two sold for upwards of $80 each in Europe, while the Hourglass was only $25. So demure, so inviting was the Hourglass that buyers—including men for their ladies—stormed the stores. The design squeezed the waist and accented the hips in a most wonderful way. The acetate satin Lastex from which it was made only heightened the allurement. The secret of the design was waist boning and "bouncy bloomers" shaped to the "extravagant curves of an Edwardian hourglass."[18] European designers were entirely eclipsed.

Rose Marie's own press release reveals some idea of her thinking at the time. "Every design began with an intimate bra ingeniously devised to compensate a small bust or to accommodate a full one and to flatter in either case. In cutting the swimsuit, she introduced the device of reverse grains, working the stretchability of the lastex fabrics in reverse patterns to provide elasticity or rigidity as needed throughout the body of the suit. Added to this was an inner panel which provided genuine girdle control from within so that the ulti-mate effect was that of a one piece foundation garment actually designed into the swimsuit."[19] Shape assurance was something new to swimsuit markets. When blended with a flair for high fashion and dozens of unseen but certainly felt innovations for fit adjust-ment, the effect was like magic. She called it "magic length," and interestingly it was this very principle that startled the swimmers at the Crystal Pool in Vancouver when Jack Reid wore her very first creation. It laced up the sides so that the fit was tight no matter who was wearing the suit.

The Hourglass, with its boned and bloomered maillot, swept America overboard into Rose Marie's own little lifeboat. During its first year she shattered sales records everywhere. In 1952, sales soared to $5,000,000. Two plants were operating, one in Los Angeles and another in Montreal, turning out 1,000 suits a day.[20] Indeed, the stars literally fell for Rose Marie. Marilyn Monroe gave Rose Marie "almost as much credit as Mother Nature for her pinup popularity." Joan Crawford, Jane Russell, and Rhonda Fleming each used her suits in movies.[21]

The spinoff from the Hourglass was the Doubloon. It featured elasticized taffeta and Bengaline fabrics that were made colorfast by a Celaperm finish. The same bloomer bottoms accompanied by delicate embroidery to accent the bustline continued to capture buyers into 1954. Rose Marie widened the suit just under the arms, creating an optical illusion that "narrows anyone's waistline down to a doll-sized" miniature. To widen the hips she gave the suit pockets, set in a "wide hip-wrapping band which successfully flattens your tummy and makes your waist disappear."[22]

Rose Marie was an expert saleswoman. She pleaded with buyers to protect the new fabrics from the salt and chlorine. It was not that they could not wear them swimming, but that salt and chlorine needed to be washed out to hold the suit's color and shape. "What you really need," she continued, "is a new suit for sunning, last's year's for swimming and an extra one just for fun. A wardrobe of three or four suits isn't at all unusual any more, . . . and some women buy 12 or 13 at a time."[23] The November 1954 *Harper's Bazaar* featured her "Jewels of the Sea" collection, the same as the Lord and Taylor windows, with these alluring tidbits: "From Trinidad to Tuscan, Majorca to Miami, you're a part of the fun . . . if you're wearing a Rose Marie Reid original.' 'If' you've caught the 'new shape.' 'If' your 'first flight is in fashion.'"[24]

Harper's continued the Rose Marie Reid worship the next season with a full-color picture of a one-piece maillot that had a two-piece look. Made of acetate and cotton woven with Lastex, the suit illustrated Rose Marie's continuing concern for durability and style, while continuing to cover America's then modest women. Fay Hammond, a fashion writer who adored the Rose Marie Reid look, wrote, "One beautiful new rose is easy to identify this year. Just look at the label on your favorite bathing suit!"[25] When trying to recapture the "Golden Years," Marian Hall of the L. A. Fashion Group, Inc., wrote in 1976 that Rose Marie "became noted for dress-sized swimwear with the seduction of an evening gown, 'cocktail swimsuits' of gold lame, metallics, velvets, exotic fabrics the majority of swim suit manufacturers scoffed at but the customers flocked to buy."[26]

Rose Marie stayed true to her belief that "a woman looks and feels her best when she is wearing an evening dress." It was her

The LDS Relief Society ladies sewed sequins on thousands of
swimsuits to help raise money for the Los Angeles Temple.

whole philosophy: "I wanted that same feeling in a bathing suit,"
she said.

In 1955, production reached 5,000 suits a day. By 1959 they
would be producing 10,000 suits a day. The figure always startled
and amazed her, and she constantly checked the figures with the Los
Angeles sales department to be sure they were right. "I have
designed every stitch our firm has ever turned out, and I still cannot
believe the volume," she once said. Their worldwide distribution

then reached into 46 countries, which made them the largest manufacturer of ladies' swimsuits in the world.

Nor could Rose Marie believe that she was indeed "famous." Her daughter Carole recalled how as they drove along Wilshire Boulevard, passing billboards that advertised her mother's swimsuits, Rose Marie would say, "I can't believe that's me."

A fascinating story surrounds what was loosely called, inside the factory, "the Relief Society suit." Rose Marie had designed a beautiful, tight-fitting white Lastex suit with lovely striped lines accenting the contour of the waist and hips, which required the sewing on of thousands of brightly colored sequins, however. The Mormon Church was then building its Los Angeles temple, and the local members were very involved in fund raising for the sacred building. The women's organization of the Church (Relief Society) wanted a project to help contribute to the building fund, so they approached Rose Marie to see if she had anything they could do. She allowed them to sew on the sequins, so hundreds of women donated thousands of hours sewing on sequins. Rose Marie, in turn, donated their wages to the temple fund.

The suit sold for $50 and was very popular. The story behind its success was carried in *Life* magazine.[27] Among those who wore the suit publicly were Marcia Valibus, Miss Miami Beach of 1959; and actress Terry Moore, who modeled the swimsuit as the one she chose to wear on her honeymoon with her husband, Eugene C. McGrath, a Panama City insurance broker. The suit also appeared on Carol Anders in an exclusive Beverly Hills Hilton Hotel fashion show, and on Marie Hermann, queen of the Los Angeles press photographers. Sandy Rosten wore it in Puerto Rico with the Martha Rae traveling troupe at a Marine Corps USO production. And it was seen on the Phil Silvers show when the comical Sergeant Bilko plotted with his men in a scheme to fill the empty suit with a girl. But the suit never got as much attention as it did from Georgia Poulos in Bridgeport, Mississippi, in a Miss Universe audition. Miss Poulos modeled the suit in the swimsuit competition but was disqualified when they discovered she had stolen it off a mannequin at a local department store. Miss Poulos tearfully explained that she hadn't the money to buy a suit for the competition, and everyone knew whoever wore this suit would win.

The genius behind Rose Marie's designing was her belief that fashion required honest-to-goodness "engineering," which she recoined "imagineering." Her theory was to shape the swimsuit to the woman, camouflaging from the outside while constructing a foundation garment from the inside. This philosophy left no consideration for the bikini, and she almost single-handedly "booted the bikini" onto the back burner during the fifties.

The bikini controversy ultimately proved to be the end of her affiliation with the swimsuit industry, but in 1956 she had her way. The *Boston Record* praised her for making "discretion the better part of THE SHOW" and doing it with fashion and color. According to the *Record's* fashion editor, "When it comes right down to it, cotton's real claim to fame and fit of the swimsuit has always been a matter of print and pattern rather than the fashion and fit of the swimsuit itself. In analyzing the cotton picture, Rose Marie Reid found that an overwhelming majority of cotton suits were minimum coverage shirred-back sheaths which are wonderful for young girls with good figures, but which left a lot to be desired for the woman with a few problems they don't care to reveal at the beach."[28] Rose Marie solved the problem by broadening women's choices.

The latter fifties saw only increases in the volume of sales and the clear superiority of Rose Marie's designs over her competition. In 1957, *Vogue* carried a full-page ad featuring the new "Ansonia" elasticized fabric. The suit was entitled "More Magic," and all agreed that Rose Marie was the leader.

In 1958, knits came to the fore. It was a full circle for her, for the very suits that were hated so much in the thirties were of heavy knit, having no form or fit. Rose Marie urged her buyers to "pay as much attention to the figure control features of knit . . . as they have learned to insist on in swimsuits of Lastex." This time the knits were lovely in color and weave and responded to the figure-molding features common to all Reid suits. Rose Marie also carried eight chemise suits in her line that year. "The chemise makes most women look younger," said Rose Marie.[29] And America's women responded by buying them in railroad car lots.

During 1958, the simple swimsuit blossomed into a wardrobe. *The Dallas Times-Herald* featured Rose Marie in early June displaying the accessory line that now was deemed a necessity by every well-dressed beach goer. "Instead of a single suit she has a wardrobe. And each suit is part of a costume, complete from head to toe," said Graydon Heartstill of the *Herald*. And Rose Marie was there—the best with the most. Accessory lines included straw hats, headbands, and lipstick and eyeshadow color-coordinated to the headband, "enough color to set the beach ablaze," said Heartstill.[30] Out of five suits featured on the front page of the fashion section of the Columbus, Ohio *Citizen* for the week of June 8, four of the suits were Rose Marie Reid's.

One newspaper summarized Rose Marie's effect on the identity for 1958 as follows: "Rose Marie Reid retraces history as far back as the Renaissance period to carry the mood for her brocades for the beach. Calling them 'glowing reflections of a golden era,' she has designed shimmering silhouettes eloquently cast on fabrics 'that speak of tapestried castles and queens.'"[31]

Rose Marie was the darling of the era. The American Sportswear Design Awards, sponsored by *Sports Illustrated*, nominated her the designer of the year.[32] *The California Stylist* said of her designs in a fifteen-page feature article, this the "strongest swimsuit line in our history."[33] The *Stylist* claimed to have over 55 million reader impressions to back up the claim.

An article titled "Brains, Beauty and Bathing Suits" in *This Week* magazine stated, "Recently a hundred UCLA co-eds were asked what trade name they know best and they answered, 'Rose Marie Reid.' In five years, swim togs designed by Rose Marie Reid have revolutionized the bathing suit business and skyrocketed Rose Marie Reid to the top of the trade. . . . Her factory is the largest, most modern apparel factory on the west coast."[34]

The decade ended with Rose Marie strongly voicing her opposition to the coming bikini onslaught. The *Saint Petersburg Times*, calling her "Neptune's Designing Daughter," shows Rose Marie gallantly affirming that there will be "no future for the bikini in America."[35] In truth, she really believed that American women wanted more than to expose their bodies to the public. She felt that the refinement and loveliness of women, wives, and daughters would be paramount in the desires of their husbands and fathers; for everyone knew, especially women, that part of the feminine mystique was a little mystery and certainly modesty.

Notes

1. Bosker and Lencek, "In the Swim," *Alaska Airlines*, p. 31.
2. Ibid.
3. Ibid.
4. Ibid.
5. Marjorie Griswald, letter to Rose Marie Reid, n.d.
6. Marjorie Griswald, letter to Rose Marie Reid, n.d.
7. Marjorie Griswald Deposition, 9 September 1955, Docket No. 51225.
8. Rose Marie Reid, letter to Marion Heilner, n.d.
9 Jane Allen, *The Oregonian*, 15 June 1948, p. 16.
10. Ibid.
11. *San Francisco Examiner*, 8 May 1950, p. 21.
12. Ibid.
13. *Esquire*, February 1951.
14. *Life*, July 1952, p. 67.
15. Rose Marie Reid, letter to Marion Heilner, n.d.
16. Ibid.
17. Marjorie Griswald, letter to Rose Marie Reid, n.d.
18. *Life*, July 1952, p. 67.
19. Rose Marie Reid, advertising brochure, 1952
20. *Vancouver Sun*, 10 October 1953, p. 19.
21. Ibid.
22. *Miami Daily News*, 28 January 1954, p. 4-B.
23. Ibid.
24. *Harper's Bazaar*, November 1954, p. 48.
25. Hammond, "Miss Reid Suits Swimmer Best," *Los Angeles Times*.
26. Marion Hall, "The Golden Years," a pamphlet prepared by the L.A. Fashion Group, 1976, p. 29.
27. *Life*, July 1952, p. 67.
28. *Boston Record*, 3 May 1956.
29. *Boston Evening American*, 1 July 1958, p. 32.
30. Graydon Heartsill, *Dallas Times-Herald*, 8 June 1958.
31. Unidentified, undated newspaper clipping in author's possession.
32. *The Utah Peace Officer*, June 1959, p. 9.
33. *California Stylist*, May 1958, p. 19.
34. *This Week*, September 1951, p. 8-10
35. *Saint Petersburg Times*, 30 May 1958.

CHAPTER 11

Rose Marie Reid, Mormon Missionary

One of Rose Marie's friends, Dean Olson, the mayor of Beverly Hills, said, "I have found that when I tell the people with whom I'm doing business that I am a Mormon, the whole character of our relationship changes, for they then feel that they can trust me, that my word is my bond, that there is something about being a Mormon that sets me apart from any other business association. . . . My being a Mormon has been a great asset."[1]

Like Dean, Rose Marie was proud to declare her religion. When she was selected as one of ten Women of the Year in 1955 by the *Los Angeles Times*, she responded to the interviewer, "We're Mormons, you know."[2]

Rose Marie never missed an opportunity to say, "I am a Mormon, and this is what Mormons believe." As her fame and exposure grew, she found she was in demand all over the world, not only for her designs but also for personal appearances and interviews. The more visible she became, the more opportunity she had to explain her philosophy of life, especially her belief in God and the restored gospel of Jesus Christ.

Rose Marie spoke to every associate, employee, reporter, repairman, banker, fabric manufacturer, airline stewardess, fellow passenger, friend, neighbor, telephone operator, and relative. She spoke to her relatives' friends and her children's friends as well. She found that because she was who she was, all would listen to what she had to say. Rose Marie felt that the most important thing she had to tell them was a truth more critical and needed than any comment on fashion design. To create opportunities to explain her religion, Rose Marie always responded to introductions with a comment such as this: "Thank you, but I believe God has made my success possible. Did you know I am a Mormon?" And then she would tell them about her religion. Because of her enthusiasm and genuineness, people enjoyed learning about her religious beliefs.

Rose Marie lamented that one time while she was on a flight to the East coast, she didn't have her missionary materials as she usually did. She declared, "I am never going to travel without all my missionary equipment again. I sat by a man on the plane—the only vacant seat—and as we left L. A. and got immediately into the desert, he said, 'Imagine our forefathers crossing this desert in covered wagons.' And I said, 'Imagine the Mormon pioneers, wagons and handcarts.' And he said, 'Do you know much about Mormons? I'd like to get a book about them.' What a door to open to me! He had never joined a church but he and his wife go to church every Sunday. . . . He'd read the Bible and couldn't understand why preachers always read a passage from the Bible and then say, 'Now this interpreted means something else.'"

Even though she had no materials, Rose Marie taught him as best she could. When he expressed his feelings that no one had the authority to baptize in this day and age, Rose Marie explained the Apostasy and the Restoration of the church of Jesus Christ upon the earth through the prophet Joseph Smith. The man's response was, "If you could show me that Mormons have authority from God, my wife and I would submit to baptism so fast, because we know it's essential."

After the plane landed in Florida, Rose Marie arranged for the local missionaries to visit him immediately. She visited him as well during her next trip to Florida. To Marion she concluded: "It all shows how well the Lord manages after one of his blessings [her ordination as a missionary] has been given. He just opens doors for me, and I dare not keep quiet. I looked at that man when I first sat down and thought, 'I'm not going to speak a word to you. I have writing and reading to do,' and then I started him on the road to conversion."[3]

Mormon historian Cleon Skousen recalled that Rose Marie had invited him and his wife, Jewel, to Sardi's Restaurant. Many influential Jewish businessmen were a part of their dinner party that evening. Somehow in the course of the evening, a question came up about her religion. Cleon said, "I watched as she cleared away the crystal goblets and the china and wrote right on the fine linen tablecloth, explaining the whole history of Judah and Joseph as sons of Jacob. There in the presence of those influential people, on which her livelihood depended, she taught them eloquently," said Brother Skousen.[4]

Rose Marie's daughter Carole describes how one of her friend's father came to pick up his daughter from a visit with Carole. "Before he left, my mother had engaged him in a conversation about the Church, [and] they scheduled a return visit [for his family] to come back to the house and learn more. In a few months they were baptized."

Rose Marie always invited the children's friends to Church youth activities, and many joined the Mormon Church. Those who didn't still maintained high regard for Rose Marie and her beliefs. Thirty years after associating with the family, Bruce's friend Luther Hussey still has "a great deal of fondness for and respect for the people," adding that "it was very impressive the way Rose Marie Reid took such an interest in church that she would go out and work on the welfare farms. So did the kids. . . . Rose Marie's family always had hope for us 'sinners' across the street. We weren't converted Mormons yet, so they never gave up on trying for us. We never quite made it." Nevertheless, Luther received visits from the missionaries and helped out at the church in Westwood, "crawling among the rafters . . . trying to do some useful work. It was a lot of fun. Except for a few questions that bothered me, I became very close to being a Mormon."

Luther did some work at the film vaults in Salt Lake City, working for a company building film processors. "It was at that time the largest film vault for a nongovernmental agency in the world," recalled Luther. "It had about a million rolls of film. Certainly the help I got from Church members was the best. They did everything I asked them to do and then some." Of Rose Marie's family, Luther said, "It's been a very nice thing knowing one Mormon family very well."

Dorothy Cox, Rose Marie's friend and business associate from Canada, once tearfully called Rose Marie and told her of her impending divorce and loneliness. Rose Marie felt that the gospel of Jesus Christ would give Dorothy hope and comfort in her anguish and pain. "Come to Los Angeles and stay with us," Rose Marie invited her. While Dorothy visited with her, Rose Marie taught her the gospel and gave her a position working beside her in the company. Dorothy joined the Mormon Church and sent for her two children. A talented seamstress and designer, Dorothy soon married a faithful Mormon man in the temple. Her son served a mission for the Church in Australia, and later became a stake mission president.

Carole remembers vividly walking into Mother's room one day as she was having a telephone conversation. "Of course it was a gospel discussion," Carole laughed as she recalled the incident. Knowing that her mother was on an international call, which was an unusual thing in those years, Carole thought the conversation rather lengthy for such a long distance. "[Mother] later told me the call was difficult to get through, and the conversation she was having was with the operator assisting her. Before the call was completed, she had this operator's name and address for the missionaries in her area and had set up an appointment." Carole remembers thinking to herself, "Only my mother would do that!" Carole later met that operator when she visited with Rose Marie Reid in their home.

One day, two Mormon missionaries knocked at the door of Helen King, who lived just up the street from Rose Marie. "Do you know Rose Marie Reid, the famous swimsuit designer?" they asked Helen. "She is a Mormon and she lives here on the same block."

No, Helen replied, she didn't know her since she always kept to herself. But she was curious to know who this famous person was. Only a few days later, Helen received a carefully handwritten note inviting her over to Rose Marie's mansion just down the street. (The missionaries had contacted Rose Marie and asked her to contact Helen.) Helen's curiosity was piqued, and she responded to the invitation.

When she knocked on the door, Rose Marie herself answered the door, wearing a pretty black dress with a white starched apron. Helen's first thought to herself was "My heavens, how does one get a maid like this?!"

Rose Marie greeted her cordially, and a friendship was struck that would last until Rose Marie's death. The two were always at each other's back doors, sharing some personal experiences or some delicious treat Helen had prepared. When fresh bread came from the oven in Rose Marie's house, usually of Marie's making, Rose Marie would call Helen, who would come over, and the two friends would dine on fresh bread and butter.

Recognizing that Rose Marie was very busy, Helen volunteered to assist her with entertaining. When distinguished persons came to Rose Marie's home, Helen planned the menu and assisted in the preparation of the meal. She also loaned Rose Marie all of her beautiful silver serving pieces. Helen said her neighbors often asked her why she was constantly taking things from Rose Marie's house, since they saw her carrying things back and forth. Little did they realize that Helen was almost always taking her beautiful things to Rose Marie's. One spring, Helen told Rose Marie, "It isn't right—a woman of your station not having proper things. I'm going to New York and Europe, and I'll get you everything you need to entertain properly!"

True to her word, Helen carefully selected wonderful linens and silver, crystal vases, and a dozen other items. Rose Marie gratefully accepted it all and happily paid the bill. "She made certain Mother was a proper hostess," said Sharon.

Helen accompanied Rose Marie to speaking engagements; since Helen was Jewish, the two had lengthy discussions while traveling. "She taught me every chance she had; every moment we were together she was teaching me," said Helen. "My friends and family were the first to see how she had changed my life and would always comment 'We are so happy to see that some of Rose Marie has rubbed off on you.' I can only say Amen and thank our dear God for sending her my way."[5]

Helen wanted to be baptized but was concerned about disappointing her family and friends. For some people the decision to join the Church was simply too difficult. But Rose Marie's love was never conditional upon anyone's membership in the Church. She valued all people.

Although Rose Marie was busy with new friends, she still remembered the many wonderful friends she had left behind in Canada. Since the business could not continue manufacturing there, she still felt a continued responsibility for them. A janitor at her Canadian factory carried on a dialogue with her about the Church by mail for years.

Bob Marcou, the manager of the Canadian plant, also kept a relationship by mail with her for years. They debated business and religion continually. After reading from the early Christian fathers— Pliny, St. Polycarp, Euseubius—as well as the writings of Josephus and a newly discovered Greek manuscript of the Bible, Bob was convinced that the Apostasy from the early Christian church that Rose Marie had told him about could not have occurred as early as Rose Marie said. Aware of some early Christians who delayed baptism until just before death so as to ensure them—so they believed— entrance into the kingdom of heaven, Bob wrote to Rose Marie: "Perhaps my smoking and drinking could be so absolved."[6]

Though Rose Marie would not let him get away with this line of thinking, she enjoyed her dialogue with him about his readings. "I loved your articles, as you knew I would," she wrote. "I also believed them. I was interested in the article by Dr. John Trooyer who belonged to a mystical sect who believed that the universe is populated with invisible spirits, good and bad, who influence the lives of human beings. How near some beliefs come to the same truths. Showing that they all had a common source way back beyond history, but, like the birds learning to build the nest, each left the truth at some incomplete stage and therefore are left wondering, thinking that there are no explanations for so many things of this world."[7]

Nevertheless, Rose Marie was determined to confront Bob with the *truth*. She defended the Apostasy as she had explained it to him, and told him of the mission of the Prophet Joseph Smith. As always, her style of communication was marked by her deference to the male ego, a powerful secret to her persuasive powers. To Bob, she said: "If you, who have read so much and understand so clearly, could not answer the question you asked about the Apostasy, how could the rest of the world, who are so much below you in comprehension?" Following this comment, however, her letter held two full pages of single-spaced, perfectly clear prose unequivocally explaining the Apostasy.

Bob never resolved the debate within himself, and ultimately died of acute alcoholism.

For Rose Marie, missionary work for her beliefs was almost a consuming passion. Although most Mormons have "callings" within the Church, as it is run by a lay ministry, Rose Marie was unable to hold any kind of position that required regular Sunday attendance because of her extensive travel related to her business. Her missionary work became so well known in Los Angeles that the Los Angeles stake mission president, Orson Haney, recognizing her unique capability for missionary work, said to her, "You ought to be made a missionary so that you can do missionary work wherever you are."[8] He suggested that she be officially "set apart," which refers to the formal act of receiving authority from presiding leaders to fulfill certain duties.

Rose Marie was set apart on 26 April 1953. In anticipation of this event, she wrote to Marion: "I'm to be set apart as a missionary on Apr. 26 [1953]. *Do not tell anyone.* Mother preferred for it not to be official. Besides, I can do more unofficially."[9]

It is particularly interesting to note that Rose Marie made the following comment to Marion: "Divorces didn't matter." This reveals how Rose Marie continued to perceive her own status in the Church as not quite acceptable. Her missionary efforts were perhaps in part an attempt to make up for what she saw as a personal failure because of her unsuccessful marriages. Later, she would write to Marion, "I feel so self-conscious about my unmarried state." Although she commented, "Maybe no one thinks of it," she also wondered if her marital status ultimately led her church leaders to lose confidence in the missionary lessons she later created.[10]

Rose Marie remained an official missionary for the Mormon Church until she left California in the early 1970s. She was even given special permission to do missionary work alone when no companion was available to accompany her. (Ordinarily, missionaries teach in pairs.)

Her calling as a missionary was very important to Rose Marie. She would have given all her time and money to the Church, and in fact gave half a million dollars to Brigham Young University (which was equal to approximately five million dollars in 1994); she gave hundreds and thousands more in tithes and offerings. But she well knew the Lord required more than money. Paul Haberfield, manager of Rose Marie's factory, once asked: "Do you have to give so much time to your church?" Rose Marie's answer was a simple "Yes!"

She felt her home was a gift from the Lord. She used it extensively for entertaining dignitaries, and she frequently taught the gospel there. Because of its proximity to the temple, it was an ideal place for teaching the proud populace of Los Angeles. Many of those she taught were accomplished and affluent—a humble cottage would not have attracted them.

Rose Marie also garnered many lasting friends among the Church leadership. Elder LeGrand Richards, one of the General Authorities of the Church and one of the greatest missionaries in the history of the Church, came to be one of her close friends. She often expressed to him her sorrows and her happiness with the work, and in turn, Elder Richards shared his concerns through their correspondence. Of great concern to him was the trend to baptize people without taking time to truly teach and convert them. In one letter to Rose Marie, he shared her negative reaction to some material prepared by the stake mission president, who had written, "Your area, your district, and your region . . . all are to be perfectly united in a single, concerted unified drive for baptisms." Not once, said Elder Richards, had the mission president made any reference to conversions.[11]

Rose Marie shared his concern over this observation and replied, "I loved your letter. I hope in all my life, in all I do, it will always be in as complete agreement with your thinking as it is in this letter." The missionary plan set a date for baptism at "the very first meeting," and Rose Marie wondered, "'But when do they learn the gospel?' Mission presidents have replied, 'After they are in the Church.' And I say, 'Not in Sunday School, there is not time. Not in sacrament meeting; for too many, very little is retained of what is heard there.'"[12]

As a member of a church that was just beginning to emerge into the world arena, Rose Marie was frustrated with the common acceptance that "growth" was synonymous with "good." Since the Church had been held back and had lived under the clouds of persecution for a long time, Church leaders and mission presidents throughout the world wanted numerous conversion stories to tell at general conference and to publish in the *Church News*. The Church had a prophet in David O. McKay, who looked like a modern Moses, newly arisen to divide the Red Sea of negative world opinion. Temples in London, Switzerland, and Los Angeles served as beacons to the world that Latter-day Saints were a force to be reckoned with. It was a new day for the Church, like no other ever known.

To Elder Richards, Rose Marie revealed her concerns that baptisms were valued over conversions. "Oh, I do not say these things to other people anymore, for it sounds too much like I am finding fault with those in authority, and I have been taught all my life how wrong that is, so the fault I am complaining about is not as big as mine is when I complain. So I stop. So only your eyes must ever see this, for I know you understand."[13]

Rose Marie desired people to accept baptism, but she was not one to compromise; she wanted conversions, not just baptisms. New members, she believed, had to be taught carefully and taught an altogether new way of loving people. To ensure that converts were assimilated into the ward family, she wrote instructions to the bishops on how to integrate new members. Her approach was in such demand that she printed a pamphlet with her suggestions. Certainly, she acknowledged, fellowshipping, supporting, and including new members was important to their continued growth in the Church. But she also felt that honesty, integrity, and adherence to the teachings themselves were important so that life-long members would never offend those who sought and needed examples of righteous Latter-day Saint living.

Like a skirted Joshua, Rose Marie Reid heralded truth pure and undefiled—the people listening to her message felt her pure testimony and longed after its source. She purchased hundreds of copies of the Book of Mormon, missionary Bibles, and Elder Richards' book, *A Marvelous Work and A Wonder*, to give to her contacts.

Each had pertinent passages underlined and commentary written in the margins. Rose Marie's mother said to Marion, "Her harvest is growing for sure!"[14] In her files are lists of people she taught and lists of other missionaries she trained—seven full pages of names. When her daughter Carole asked her in 1958 how many people she had taught who were baptized, Rose Marie estimated that it was over one hundred. Carole felt it was closer to several hundred.

Not everyone she taught joined the Mormon Church, but all were appreciative of her sincere desire to help and to improve lives through the gospel message. One person who listened to her teachings painted a beautiful oil portrait of the Prophet Joseph Smith dressed all in white, and gave it to Rose Marie as a tribute to her beliefs and compassion for others. John Rastello appreciated her teachings as well, and wrote to thank her: "I am a Catholic but I have never spoken or been present at such a gathering and heard a speaker with the faith and humility that you demonstrated."[15] Others sent notes of thanks for her good Christian instruction. One individual from San Diego wrote: "In these last years my convictions have rocked to the extremes! . . . [But] one simply could not walk away without being convinced. . . . You are one of the few who lives completely . . . your belief."[16] There were hundreds of similar responses.

After Rose Marie spoke at a business meeting, Stan Zundell, an executive with the Bank of America in Santa Monica, California, wrote her on 27 July 1955: "I just couldn't let this opportunity go by to tell you . . . how much your sweet little talk meant to me personally. I have been brought up in the Mormon tradition as my grandfather was one of the pioneers who helped settle the West. I have always loved the Gospel—and needed it.

"But quite often my faith has wavered—and at no time in my life had it been at such low ebb as the morning of your talk. I consider it a minor miracle that I attended the meeting. I hadn't intended to do so—but peculiar circumstances brought me there.

"Truthfully, I didn't see your models nor your swim suits. I only heard what you said about Mormonism—and the way you said it. If an angel had come down straight from Heaven . . . , I couldn't have been more impressed. I came away from the meeting with my heart singing—because I need the Gospel, badly. I'm lost without it—yet,

I often have a hard time believing—just believing. . . . I believe you are the very best missionary Mormonism could have."

Because she cared so deeply about the restored gospel of Jesus Christ, Rose Marie was frustrated by Church members who were careless with new converts in any way. For instance, one member who held an important position in the Church borrowed money from her, and refused to repay it. When she said, "It has been several years since I loaned you that $40,000, and I have a child who needs it right now," his reply was, "I thought you understood the Lord gave you that money to *give* to me." Rose Marie wondered how many people he had obtained money from using this sort of argument, that he could give such an answer "with a clean conscience."[17]

Rose Marie feared for new members who might come into contact with such Mormons. Once a Russian couple who had immigrated to the United States and joined the Church lived in her ward. The husband was a janitor, and the wife held two domestic jobs. When Rose Marie noticed that the husband no longer came to church, she asked his wife if her husband was ill. The woman began to cry, and replied in heavily accented English that a "good" Mormon had sold them a car that didn't run, and then had refused to take it back. "It took all the money we had," said the woman.

Rose Marie was furious. "Don't you realize," she said to the woman, "what will happen to that man who sold your husband a bad car? But your husband has done too much good for the gospel already to let anybody stop him, no matter who it is."[18]

Rose Marie was relieved when this humble man returned to church, and yet at the same time was frustrated with the example of the other member. Her own grandfather, Jasper Yancey, had fed and protected the missionaries in Mississippi, and then had traveled to Utah, where a Church member stole Jasper's much-needed water. To her, such action was inexcusable, especially by those who had access to the restored gospel of Jesus Christ and yet did not act in accordance with the teachings they had been given.[19]

Rose Marie Reid never hesitated to share her beliefs with others. She taught that the principles of Mormonism could be successfully used by all. As she saw the world and its desperate need for goodness, she believed the teachings of Christ were the answer. At the same time she felt that teaching encompassed a broad spectrum. Non-Mormons could help Mormons just as well and sometimes better than other Mormons.

In 1959 she invited Georgiana Hardy, president of the Los Angeles Board of Education, to speak to an all-Mormon group. Georgiana, whose son was an Episcopalian minister, said to the gathering, "I am convinced that the Lord put us on earth to be us— to be children second, to be wives second, to be parents second, to be leaders in the community second, whatever it may be. You have nothing to contribute to husbands, children, parents, Sunday School, community or anything else unless you are a person, a person living up to his best potential."[20] Rose Marie knew that every Mormon could benefit from this advice, and she wanted this growth for more than just herself. Few others in the Mormon community could have obtained Georgiana's acceptance to give such a speech, but Rose Marie could. So she did.

Rose Marie, of course, wanted everyone to join the Mormon Church; but most of her close associates were not Mormons, so she learned from them and taught them just as readily.

Notes

1. Dean Olson, speech given at Brigham Young University, May 1959; quoted in Rose Marie Reid's speech to Brigham Young University students in June 1959.
2. Hammond, "Miss Reid Suits Swimmer Best," *Los Angeles Times.*
3. Rose Marie Reid, letter to Marion Heilner, 15 March 1963 (Salt Lake City).
4. Cleon Skousen, interview, n.d.
5. Helen King, interview, 1 March 1990. All subsequent comments from Helen King are taken from this source.
6. Bob Marcou, letter to Rose Marie Reid, 7 & 16 December 1953.
7. Rose Marie Reid, letter to Bob Marcou, December 1953 (Los Angeles, California).
8. Rose Marie Reid, Oral History, p. 110.
9. Rose Marie Reid, letter to Marion Heilner, n.d.
10. Rose Marie Reid, letter to Marion Heilner, 17 September 1961.
11. LeGrand Richards, letter to Rose Marie Reid, 15 March 1963.
12. Rose Marie Reid, letter to LeGrand Richards, n.d.
13. Rose Marie Reid, letter to LeGrand Richards, 20 March 1963 (Los Angeles, California).

14. Marie Yancey, letter to Marion Heilner, n.d.

15. John Rastells, letter to Rose Marie Reid, 20 November 1958.

16. M. B. L., letter to Rose Marie Reid, 30 October 1953 (San Diego, California).

17. Rose Marie Reid, Oral History, p. 101

18. Ibid., p. 102

19. Ibid.

20. Georgiana Hardy, manuscript of speech, n.d.

A California garden dinner with (left to right) Carole, Rose Marie, Bruce, Nina and Jack Kessler, and Sharon (front)

CHAPTER 12

Mother to All

Along with her beliefs and her devotion to missionary work, Rose Marie's life was her children. When asked about her "hobbies," she exclaimed, "Hobbies? My children are my hobbies. . . We discuss all the girl-friend and boy-friend problems as well as lessons, too."[1]

When Rose Marie was interviewed by *New Liberty* magazine she was asked, "What is your favorite orchestra?"

She replied, "The kindergarten rhythm band when my son played the triangle."[2] She wanted more than anything to see her children grow up doing good things, and she hung on every good thing they did. To Marion she wrote in 1953, "Bruce . . . was best in his class!"[3]

Rose Marie always made it a point to teach her children that adherence to their religious beliefs was more important than money. In the numerous speeches that Rose Marie gave to church and business groups, she would tell how an advertising opportunity worth $250,000 once came her way just as the California company was starting up. Jack Kessler telephoned her in Vancouver, where the family was still living while Rose Marie was commuting to Los Angeles. Kessler told Rose Marie that "a very large company wants to use you in their advertising. They want to know when you will be back in New York for the photographs."

Rose Marie said, "Tell them I'll go any time for that."

Then Jack said, "There is only one hitch in it. You have to say that you smoke Camel cigarettes."

Rose responded, "Oh, my goodness! Well, ask if I can say Camels must be the best because my partner smokes them."

"No," said Jack, "the slogan is 'Experience is the best teacher,' and so they want you, and *you* have to say that."

Rose Marie answered, "Well, Jack, you know the answer. I couldn't possibly."

Jack told her not to answer right away. He'd call her the next day after she had thought it over.

Said Rose Marie later, "Well, our budget for advertising that year—that we could afford to spend ourselves—was about $30,000. So to get $250,000 worth of advertising free would have been tremendous." That night at home, Rose Marie asked her children, who were seven, nine and eleven, "How would you like to have someone advertise our business for us so we would have lots of money and we could buy a big beautiful home with a swimming pool, and cars, and a horse for Bruce to ride, and everything you want?"

And they said, "Oh, Mommy, how?"

"A company wants to use me in its advertising. All I have to do is say I smoke Camel cigarettes."

The children responded in disgust, "'Oh, Mommy, we don't need a swimming pool."[4]

The children for the most part were protected from the business worries of their mother. "We knew very little about how hard it was and how much courage it took to become a successful business woman. We thought she could do anything and that she could make all things possible," said Carole.

When the need arose, Rose Marie could discipline quite effectively in a calm, even voice. This calm was a treasured gift that the children remembered later in life. "She could look crushed, until I would give anything for her to spank me rather than look so crushed," said Sharon. "If anything really went wrong—broken bay window or a smashed car, a broken filter on the pool from carelessness—she would just talk to us, ask what had happened and how we felt about it, and that was all. And that was enough."

Rose Marie always came home from work happy. Before arriving home she would stop along the highway, put on her makeup, take one of her short naps and refresh herself for the children. Her financial concerns were very seldom shared with them, except to ask them to pray for one line or another.

"We had a constant faith in a Father in Heaven, which she instilled in us," said Carole. Though they didn't have a father in the home, Rose Marie always taught them of a Father in Heaven. "We could always depend on him, and as children, we always did."

Rose Marie taught her children gifts of charity and frugality. She herself made her own clothing, patterned after the clothing exhibits she had carefully observed in the fashionable store windows. "She was never excessive," said Carole. Furthermore, she continued, "clothes that didn't get worn, were given away." If the children didn't wear certain items of clothing, they were bundled up and given to family or to others.

Every year when Rose Marie's family visited from Idaho, Rose Marie outfitted them all with their school clothing. Carole was put in charge of the shopping expeditions.

By treating her children as adults, Rose Marie taught them to be superbly independent. When Carole was twelve years old, she was already mature beyond her years; she traveled to New York City and stayed alone in a hotel for a month. She saw every play on Broadway and visited every sight.

"It never occurred to me I was too young or not competent enough to be there alone," Carole said. "Taxis took me everywhere I needed to go. . . . I knew the Rose Marie Reid offices were close by on Broadway if I needed anything. Thinking back, I never hesitated going; but I would never permit my own twelve-year-old children such a venture."

Sharon left home to complete her high school education at the Annie Wright Seminary, a prestigious private school in Tacoma, Washington. Rose Marie allowed it only because Sharon thought it best. Sharon had carefully evaluated her needs and presented a plan to her mother, who then carefully discussed it with her fourteen-year-old daughter and helped her carry the plan into fruition.

When Carole was barely fifteen and Bruce was seventeen, Rose Marie arranged for them to live in a small town in southern Utah where they could experience ranching and riding. Rose Marie thought it an excellent opportunity, for Bruce especially, to be a part of a normal family with a father figure and other male role models, so she sought out a family with whom they could live and Carole could attend school while Rose Marie herself traveled in Europe.

Bruce saw the uranium boom in the area and convinced his mother to let him prospect and stake some uranium claims. It never occurred to her that she should deflate his enthusiasm, so she completely outfitted him with jeep and Geiger counters, and he seriously went out to discover uranium. Once, in mid-July, Bruce and Carole took off for the remote Red Canyon area, now covered by the waters of Lake Powell. They left the road and drove deep into the red hot desert. After several hours of driving, the jeep threw a rod—they were completely stranded! They had no idea how to exactly retrace their journey through hours of unmarked terrain. The heat was excruciating, and neither was equipped with hiking gear. But they began walking, knowing that they could not simply wait for a passerby to help in the uninhabited desert.

"I cried for a while because I was afraid of snakes and centipedes," recounted Carole. "I prayed for help, thinking some parachute would come and save us, but when it didn't, I just followed Bruce, mile after mile, until we came to an old trailer, many miles away."

Bruce "hot-wired" an old jeep that was by the trailer, and they drove into the small town of Hite, Utah, dirty and tired, but relieved. It was well after midnight when they arrived. Rose Marie just considered it a learning experience. It was proof that her children were ingenious, strong, and perfectly capable to deal with anything, even the blistering sun and desert. "It gave her more pride in us," said Carole, who had begun to realize that her life had been fairly unusual. "That time," she added, "I knew we were all crazy. I still wonder what two California kids were doing out in the middle of nowhere searching for uranium."

Of all her family relationships, Rose Marie felt especially protective toward her sister Marion's daughter, Claire Rose Heilner. The only daughter in the Heilner family, Claire was beautiful and talented, much like Rose Marie herself. Rose Marie could not have loved Claire more if the girl had been her own daughter, and Claire often said she "grew up with almost two mothers."

After Claire graduated from the Annie Wright Seminary, Rose Marie insisted that she go to New York to develop her talents in music and theater, where she arranged for private vocal instruction and exposed Claire to the wonderful world of the arts.

Claire loved New York. She attended socials at Dartmouth, Yale, and Princeton, and became known for her wit and beauty. One weekend in Bermuda she met and, at nearly first sight, fell in love with a handsome young Jewish boy, Eugene Freedmon.

Although both Rose Marie and Marion were impressed with Eugene, he was not a member of their faith. Rose Marie felt she could not have their marriage "on her conscience," so she coaxed Claire to move to Los Angeles, attend UCLA, and live with her. Of course, her main objective was for Claire to become so involved with California, her schooling, acting and modeling that she would soon forget Eugene.

Claire made the move and, as Rose Marie had planned, became very involved in a flurry of activity. She studied, worked, took voice lessons, and was active in the Church.

But Eugene was not forgotten. He wrote Claire regularly and visited often. He was intelligent, charming, and resourceful, and he loved Claire. At last Rose Marie decided that her only recourse was to convert Eugene to Mormonism. Little did she know what she had undertaken.

Eugene came from a proud Jewish heritage, and his mother and father were well known in their Jewish community. But few things in life stopped Rose Marie once she set her mind to do something, and she set about with fervor to convert Eugene.

Her first step toward converting Eugene was to make sure that Claire herself was truly converted to the teachings of the restored gospel. Rose Marie invited Claire to her various missionary meetings, and soon Claire was set apart as a missionary as well.

Living and working with so many Jewish people, Rose Marie realized how much damage had been done through the years to this courageous people. There had been so much anti-Semitism in the name of Christianity that potential converts needed to reconcile their misconceptions before they would even listen to the gospel message.

Rose Marie worked day and night, studying and spending long hours on her knees in prayer. Frequently she would write her thoughts down as they came to her; several times she awakened Claire in the middle of the night to share ideas with her. Together they studied not only the Book of Mormon, but also the Bible and Jewish tradition. Of this experience Claire wrote, "It was while I was reading the Book of Mormon as I was sitting on the bed one night, a feeling of the influence of the Holy Ghost just overcame my body and I absolutely knew that I was reading pure and unadulterated truth."[5]

With the knowledge they gained of the Jewish people—particularly through their efforts to teach Eugene—the Jewish approach became the special focus of Rose Marie and Claire's missionary efforts. The first written product of this effort was a pamphlet called *Attention Israel.* Rose Marie put all of her spirit and soul into it, reasoning with her contacts why they should accept the modern prophets as descendants of Israel, including Ephraim. She took the pamphlet to UCLA and tried it out on two Jewish students, who were very impressed that this well-known woman even cared what they thought. They listened attentively and offered their sincere criticisms, which Rose Marie incorporated in her pamphlet.

According to Eugene's account, when he first showed up at the mansion to court Claire, Rose Marie met him at the door with a Book of Mormon and an invitation to the first three missionary discussions. His consent, he said later, was "my ticket to see Claire."[6]

But Eugene was not one to be bullied, no matter how persistent Rose Marie was. There were many late-night discussions with Rose Marie leading the attack. After many firesides and visits to the ward, Eugene came to realize that he was not only a missionary contact, but also a guinea pig on whom Rose Marie wanted to test her approach for teaching other Jewish people. At one point, Eugene realized that he was beginning to enjoy what he was learning about the gospel of Jesus Christ. He said, "I was fascinated by our discussions, and in a sense they sharpened my intellectual powers." But they honed Rose Marie's, as well. The sharper his responses became, the better logic she employed. However, despite her best efforts to lead him toward baptism into the Mormon Church, Eugene was determined that the only water she would get him into was her lovely swimming pool.

In the meantime, Eugene had completely charmed the entire family, including Grandma Yancey, Aunt Florence, and Carole. Young Carole had particular reason to appreciate Eugene's friendship. On one occasion, before Carole had her driver's license, she took a friend, Penny Hussey, for a drive in one of Rose Marie's Cadillacs. Returning home, she missed the swing into the driveway and crashed into the brick gatepost. Despite his own amusement, Eugene soothed her misery and took Carole with the car to be repaired.

"I remember thinking he had saved me," said Carole. "He charmed Mother out of being too upset with me [and] I knew I would not have survived without him."

When it came to the final test—whether or not he would convert to Mormonism—Eugene failed miserably to see the point of the whole effort. He really didn't care that much for any religion, including Judaism. But he loved Claire to the point of desperation, and Claire loved him.

At the same time, Rose Marie also deeply loved Claire, and she would not let Claire's life be lost outside the Mormon temple covenants. They were family, and she felt a fierce family loyalty. She pleaded with her young niece in a prayerfully written letter: "Darling, no one seemed a more positive candidate for Mormonism than your father, until the [marriage] ceremony was performed. Men have to pursue a woman. While they are in that phase [of premarital pursuit], it appeals to their manliness to have to do things to be worthy of her. At that time only will they do what she wants. And one minute after the ceremony she becomes the nagging wife when she makes the same request."[7]

At last, because of the intense pressure surrounding them, Claire and Eugene eloped in March 1955. The family was shocked, and Rose Marie was devastated. But still, she hoped Eugene would "come around" and that "maybe Claire will overcome!"[8]

Rose Marie's hopes and efforts were not in vain. Eugene had not anticipated how fiercely loyal Claire was to her religion. His hopes had been that she would move to his territory and lose her staunch commitment. Claire persistently continued to teach Eugene her beliefs, and over the years he came to appreciate the love she had for her religion. After the death of their first son from a malignant brain tumor, Eugene found the much-needed answers to his painful questions. The belief that families could be "together forever"—and live throughout eternity—rang true to him.

Soon he came to understand that Mormonism took nothing away from his Jewishness, but instead served to give him an entirely new understanding and appreciation of his heritage, along with a clear perspective of life and death. Eventually Eugene did join the Mormon Church and even became a Mormon bishop in Scarsdale, New York. His mother, ever supportive of both her children, enjoyed saying: "Who would believe I have one son that is a Jewish rabbi and another who is a Mormon bishop!"

After Eugene and Claire married and bought their new home in Scarsdale, Rose Marie came to visit. Said Claire, "She wasn't in the house five minutes before she redesigned the entire house." For the next four months, Claire and Rose Marie worked tirelessly on the house. Day after day they worked, ripping out walls, extending a porch into a large den, reupholstering furniture, hanging wallpaper, and sewing drapes, bedspreads, and pillows.

Everybody in the neighborhood knew what was going on, and they would come over daily to witness the progress. Said Claire, "We were the talk of the neighborhood. Rose Marie Reid had moved into our house, and was by her own two hands tearing down walls and redecorating and sewing and putting it back together again."

The two worked side by side. Rose Marie would awaken Claire at 5:00 a.m., and they would work nonstop until 1:00 a.m., stopping only so that Rose Marie could formulate her plans for the next day. She often sat up all night sewing.

Each morning, Eugene woke up to two new lists: things to bring home and the endless masculine chores that would await him when he returned home from work.

Rose Marie's sense of redecoration was clear genius. While reupholstering, she would rebuild couches and chairs from the base screws up to the springs, creating entirely new furniture. "Those were the days when people didn't buy great big long rods," said Claire. "Rose Marie would—in her mind—design not only the rods, which were not even sold in stores, but she would also design the patterns. My house never looked as beautiful as it did after that four months. As the years have gone by and I've had to redecorate, I have never replaced things with the kind of beautiful work that she did originally in this house."

It took Eugene a while to appreciate what these two women were doing. He felt like he was living in a cyclone, and his patience was stretched hourly. Knowing that Claire and Eugene preferred showers over bathing, Rose Marie was convinced that the bathtub in the master bathroom was not needed as much as a closet. Although Eugene resisted the idea of ripping out the bathtub, Rose Marie was convinced that once the closet was in place he would appreciate the convenience of having the extra space. Gambling on this, she waited until the family was out for an evening, then followed through with her plan. When Claire and Eugene arrived home, they found their bathtub sitting on the front lawn of their beautiful Scarsdale home. They have enjoyed the use of their closet ever since.

Eugene described his relationship with this strong-willed woman as something of a "love-hate" relationship, although later he realized that it "was more love than hate."

"Almost no one could resist her charm," he said. " I will be eternally grateful to this sensitive woman for touching my life in a positive way."

Despite her success as a designer and businesswoman, Rose Marie always said, "Family is most important." And to her daughters and other young women, she would say, "Plan on having ten children. Stay home and be a mother." This is the life Rose Marie would have chosen, but it was not the life given to her.

Still, she had "dozens of children anyway," said her daughter Sharon, "for there were always cousins and family living with us." Some came to stay the summer, others to attend UCLA; a few came to work. Rose Marie welcomed them all with open arms, never minding how many were there. Willingly and gratefully, she became their mother away from home.

In 1955 she married a third and last time to an accomplished opera singer, MacDonald Sommers. Shortly after the marriage, she learned that he already had a wife alive and well. Like Jack Reid, MacDonald joined the Church but misrepresented himself. After their divorce, Rose Marie knew she would not marry again. She never spoke of this last marriage. To her daughter Carole, she said in the last days of her life. "I never will be married, even in the celestial kingdom. I just want to be a ministering angel to you and your babies. That's all I want to be."

When speaking of her marriages she said: "I asked the Lord to make me forget. . .. The Lord let me forget . . . because he knew I couldn't stand remembering."[9]

Despite her close friendship with Ned Redding, the editor of the *California Intermountain News* and good friend of Howard W. Hunter, Rose Marie would not consent to marry again. Although Redding continued to hope that she would accept his repeated proposals, Rose Marie felt the heavy weight of the many responsibilities she had taken upon her. She also did not feel any man could accept the title of Mr. Rose Marie Reid.

For a time the three sons of Rose Marie's youngest brother, Don, came from Portland to live with Rose Marie in Los Angeles. Don was ill and experiencing difficulties in his marriage. In fact, it was Rose Marie's desire to adopt the children; but it was soon clear that the young boys found it stressful to have so many mothers— Rose Marie, Aunt Florence, Grandma Yancey, Josephine, Sharon, and Carole all tried to help them. The boys were extremely homesick and in need of personal therapy.

Rose Marie eventually helped her brother's entire family relocate to California, and she set Don up in a bookstore and a rare coin business that he could manage from his home and sickbed if necessary. "She tried with dignity to make every opportunity available for them growing up," said her daughter Sharon.

Rose Marie did not want her support to be interpreted as blatant charity; nevertheless, after Don's death, some of his family felt very bitter toward her. In fact, when Rose Marie was very ill and had been hospitalized some thirty years later, one of Don's sons telephoned her in the hospital to express his resentment at her "interference" in their lives. In Rose Marie's weakened physical condition, she found his words hurtful and even frightening.

Yes, Rose Marie could be overbearing. She often tended to delve too deeply into the lives of those she loved. But no one could doubt the depth of her sincere concern. Above all, she was a mother.

Notes

1. Hammond, "Miss Reid Suits Swimmer Best," *Los Angeles Times*.
2. *New Liberty*, 20 December 1947, p. 36.
3. Letter, Rose Marie Reid to Marion Heilner, 24 January 1953.
4. Rose Marie Reid, speech given at the Marketing Department Symposium, Brigham Young University, 1954.
5. Claire Freedmon, letter to Carole Burr, n.d.
6. Eugene Freedmon, letter, n.d. All comments by Eugene Freedmon are taken from this source.
7. Rose Marie Reid, letter to Claire Heilner, 30 October 1954.
8. Rose Marie Reid, letter to Marion Heilner, n.d.
9. Rose Marie Reid, Oral History, p. 43.

CHAPTER 13

Work Among the Jewish Community

Even before Claire had brought Eugene into the family, Rose Marie had had a special interest in the Jewish people, although she never knew that she herself had any Jewish blood in her veins. Rose Marie began focusing her missionary efforts almost exclusively toward the Jewish people, despite her backbreaking schedule—accounts in forty-six countries; manufacturing in four—Canada, Mexico, New Zealand, and Brazil; and negotiations in process for new plants in Australia, Sweden, and Holland. She saw her busy schedule as a way to bring her into contact with more people with whom to share her beliefs.

Rose Marie's love for the Jewish people was perhaps a part of her heritage. Her grandfather William Hyde's cousin was Orson Hyde, who in 1841, traveled through Europe and then overland to Palestine to dedicate Israel as a homeland for the return of the Jews. President Wilford Woodruff, president of the Church at that time, prophesied that when it was time for the Jewish people to hear the gospel and accept it, the Lord would open their hearts. Rose Marie believed that she was to follow Apostle Hyde's example of opening the way for Jewish hearts to accept the restored gospel.

Like Rose Marie, her friend Elder LeGrand Richards was also

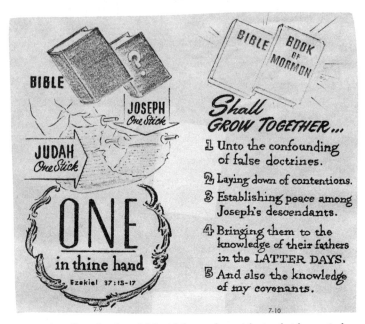

BIBLE

JOSEPH
One Stick

JUDAH
One Stick

ONE
in thine hand
Ezekiel 37:15-17

7-9

BIBLE   BOOK OF MORMON

Shall GROW TOGETHER...

1 Unto the confounding of false doctrines.

2 Laying down of contentions.

3 Establishing peace among Joseph's descendants.

4 Bringing them to the knowledge of their fathers in the LATTER DAYS.

5 And also the knowledge of my covenants.

7-10

Rose Marie formulated special Jewish lesson plans with visual aids to assist her and other missionaries. Shown here are two pages from Attention, Israel.

intrigued by the destiny and prophecies concerning the Jewish people. Thus inspired, he wrote a book called *Judah, Do You Know?* and asked Rose Marie to review it for him.

"Why not address it to Israel?" Rose Marie asked, commenting that Jewish people would be more inclined to read it. "They're all interested in the land of Israel, and everyone will read it!"[1] And so the title *Israel, Do You Know?* was born.

Elder Richards had great confidence in Rose Marie, and asked her to draft a series of lessons for the missionaries to use when approaching and teaching Jewish people. Patterning her lessons after his book, she worked from the Old Testament, discussing Judah and Joseph's relationship as brothers and sisters under the banner of ancient Jacob. She described the work of Joseph's descendants and how it would eventually culminate and join the work of Judah. She gave the Jewish people credit for the Bible, acknowledging Judah's role in preserving the "Stick of Judah" (see Ezekiel 37: 15-17).

She took this writing assignment very seriously and dedicated herself to it. She even spent some time at Murietta Hot Springs to be alone so she could write without interruption. The pamphlet *Attention Israel* was the result.

In the pamphlet, she wrote, "Here I am. What should I do? I have known from childhood that Joseph Smith was a prophet; that because he came, great and wonderful things would begin to happen. . . .[Because of this] I have greater opportunities, too, therefore greater responsibilities. I have the knowledge and opportunity to take that knowledge to the Jewish people. I don't know another person with that combination of circumstances facing them. It's no wonder I feel frightened. I'm terrified."[2]

Rose Marie believed that her talent, fame, business, money, and the setting in which she had been placed were all given her by God for this mission relating to the Jewish people. Like the Prophet Joseph Smith, she was to help fulfill the prophecy to gather home the family of Israel. As she came to understand this mission, she continually acted with it in mind. Through her involvement in the fashion industry, where she was placed in almost daily contact with some of the most influential Jewish people in the country, she taught the gospel.

Later, as she developed the actual missionary lessons, "it took a lot of coming home . . . and just going up to my room and sitting there and writing, praying, and crying," she said. But the Lord seemed to take over much of the burden. "Maybe only the Lord and I will ever know that I didn't write these lessons," she later observed. "They should only bear the Lord's byline."[3] To Rose Marie, writing was a duty, a task which she felt did not come naturally. But she had been called to the work, and she undertook it with great intensity.

Rose Marie and Jan Warner taught many people during the 1950s. Said Jan, they "were very afraid of changing, of going against family wishes, of almost being traitors. Some were even afraid to listen." But Rose Marie truly admired and loved the Jewish people, and she understood their place in history.

Rose Marie never knew that she herself had Jewish blood in her veins. Only after her death was the Jewish link discovered. Rose Marie's great-great-grandfather, Heman Hyde, had married Polly Wyman Tilton, an Algonquin Indian. The Indians inherit the blood of Judah directly from Mulek, the son of Zedekiah, the last king of Judah. The story is recorded in the Book of Mormon—the ancient book corresponding to the Bible. Following the destruction of Jerusalem by Nebuchadnezzar in 587 B.C., Mulek had come to America, where his descendants mingled their seed with that of Lehi's family. In this way, the descendants of the American Indians are a "remnant of the Jews" (see Doctrine & Covenants 19:27; see also Mosiah 25:1-2).

Rose Marie's immediate family also has Jewish blood today through marriage. Sharon Reid married Paul Alden, of Jewish descent. Rose Marie's sister, Marion, married Sanford Heilner; their daughter Claire married Eugene Freedmon, a Jewish convert to the Mormon Church. Their son, William Alan Freedmon, is promised in his patriarchal blessing that he will be among the 12,000 high priests from the tribe of Judah who will be part of the 144,000 high priests called to minister to the earth contingent to the second coming of Christ. Thus the Hyde legacy for Rose Marie and her descendants today is a blood relationship with the tribe of Judah, as well as a spiritual relationship (see Doctrine & Covenants 77).

Rose Marie spent many evenings discussing the twelve tribes of Israel with a good friend, Joseph O. Lie, who honored her with a bouquet of twelve long-stemmed roses. Said his accompanying note, "Someone said, 'Flowers speak a universal language of beauty and understanding.' So will you please accept these, one for each of the tribes of Israel, as a small token of my sincere thanks and appreciation for being allowed to share for a time your lovely family and your hopes and dreams." Lie described how he felt as he "envisioned three thousand years of history, resting on one pair of slender shoulders, and the yearning and struggle of a great people seeking prophetic solution through the efforts of one gallant heart."[4]

The Jewish people have always appreciated the importance of temples, and so at the opening of the Los Angeles Temple, Rose Marie and others organized special lectures for the large Jewish groups who visited the temple before its dedication. After the event, the Conference of Jewish Women's Organizations wrote to Rose Marie to thank her for the temple tour she had provided their nearly 1,000 members: "Your presence and aid at the entrance to the temple on the morning of the tour was indeed gracious, and your charming and informative presentation at the chapel contributed immeasurably to the success of the tour."[5] Two years later,

Rose Marie hosted the annual "Pink Tea" in her rose garden for this same Jewish women's organization. An additional 500 new members attended this lovely social at her home.

When Paul Zimmerman of Pasadena attended one of the temple tours, he introduced himself to Rose Marie. A short while later, she sent him a Rose Marie Reid rose bush (a hybrid rose created in her honor) for his garden. In reply, he wrote that he was "dogged if I know how you knew that I have a rose garden. . . . . Frankly, I can't wait for spring to start 'my' Rose Marie budding so that I can see how beautiful she really is."[6]

Rose Marie's missionary efforts toward the Jewish people are evident by her request, in 1954, for 150 copies of Elder Richard's *Israel, Do You Know?* She gave copies of Elder Richard's booklet, along with her own self-published pamphlet, *Attention Israel*, to all of her Jewish friends for their personal libraries.

From the beginning of their association, Rose Marie taught Jack and Nina Kessler, who were Jewish, about the Mormon Church. She always encouraged them to pay tithes to their own congregation, insisting that the swimsuit business would be blessed and prosper if they did. She always believed that everything belonged to the Lord, and all He asked was a tenth in return.

Rose Marie had tremendous respect for her Jewish business associates. A particular favorite was Murray Sonnet, the company salesman and distributor in Florida. Every year in January, she would present her new swimsuit line in Miami Beach. She loved visiting Murray's family and having gospel discussions. The day after one such conversation, Rose Marie wrote to Marion, Murray's wife "had a meeting with her whole family and told them about [the gospel]." Later she told Rose Marie, "'I never remember such a religious discussion before in my whole life.'"[7]

Another Jewish business associate, Eric Sorter of Soptra Fabrics, carried on a written dialogue about the Church with Rose Marie for many years. Rose Marie always gave Eric's unique fabrics the credit for the success of many of her designs. She gave Eric a copy of Elder LeGrand Richards' book, *A Marvelous Work and A Wonder*, and to the author she wrote, "Remember Mr. Sorter, of New York? . . . He wrote that he is reading *Marvelous Work* the second time, and that it is the greatest book he has ever read."[8]

In fact, while Rose Marie was in New York, Eric Sorter arranged a dinner date for her daughter Sharon with one of his friends, a nice Jewish boy from Long Island. When Rose Marie was ready to return home, Sharon begged to stay in New York. Rose Marie was not fooled. She could see the attraction between the two of them.

Sharon stayed in New York to look for a job. When she ran out of money, she called home to request more, which was exactly what her mother hoped would happen. Rose Marie wanted Sharon to come home and continue dating "good Mormon boys" so she refused to send money. However, Sharon then approached the Rose Marie Reid corporate offices, who gave her $500, thinking that Rose Marie would want them to help her daughter.

Within six weeks, Sharon and Paul Alden eloped. Although Paul was not a Mormon, Sharon insisted that he had the "Mormon look" and would some day join the Church. She read her mother's missionary lessons to Paul, and he became very interested in the concepts that were taught. He knew it would be difficult for his parents if he were baptized, so to spare them, he simply didn't tell them.

Soon after their marriage and Paul's baptism, Paul's father received the contract to do the electrical wiring on the Mormon Pavilion at the New York World's Fair. Consequently, he worked daily with several Mormon stake presidents. One of these men heard his name and said, "Aren't you Paul Alden's father?" The proud father acknowledged his son.

"Why, we baptized Paul last week," he said.

Horrified, Paul's father responded, "Not my Paul!" He would not believe his son could do such a thing, and Paul would not tell him otherwise.

After a few years, Sharon and Paul moved to Los Angeles, where Paul's parents visited them. As they happened to drive by the Mormon temple there, Paul's parents asked if Paul knew what went on inside. By this time he had been to the temple many times, and he said without thinking, "Oh, yes, I've been in there."

Shocked, his father said, "I thought you had to be a member to get in," Thinking quickly, Paul replied, "Oh, I know the right people."

Paul's mother died without ever knowing he had joined the Church, and it was eighteen years before Paul admitted it to his father.

Sharon understood that accepting the Church did not detract from Paul's Jewish heritage and was purely an extension of the great legacy and heritage his ancestors had bestowed upon him. She was proud to think that her children would share in this heritage, enhanced by the additional truths the stick of Joseph (the Book of Mormon) would bring to their lives. This, with the stick of Judah (the Old Testament), she knew contained the full truth.

Lou Tabak was another continual recipient of Rose Marie's teachings about the Mormon religion. Though he did not become a Mormon, he and Rose Marie remained good friends, and when Rose Marie's daughter Carole married, Tabak invited her to choose her whole trousseau from his wonderful line of clothing.

Harry Howard, a good friend of Rose Marie's, firmly believed that his commitment to the Mormon Church did not take away from his being Jewish. Widely respected in his community, Harry was also the president of the B'nai B'rith Lodge of the San Gabriel Valley. However, upon his baptism into the Mormon Church, the lodge members voted to oust him. Howard appealed, claiming that he was still very much Jewish, lived the faith, and therefore should not be removed from his position or from his association in the lodge. The trial attracted national attention under the banner question: "Can a Mormon Be a Jew?"

Harry contended that he merely crossed over the street to be with other Israelite brothers. "My tribe, the tribe of Judah, is so fraught with internal disorder that I merely decided to live with my cousins, the tribe of Joseph. Mormonism is a continuation of Judaism; all Jews are Israelites, but not all Israelites are Jews. Mormons are Israelites," said Harry.

When the case came up for trial, Rose Marie's lessons were cited as a defense of Howard's contentions. The newspapers reported, "As she [Rose Marie] points out, being Jewish is neither a race nor a religion, but is a genealogical bloodline from a man named Judah."[9] Harry was so grateful for her defense that he named one of his children Rose Marie in her honor.[10]

In 1953 Rose Marie met Michael Silver at a dinner party in Chicago. She found that they had much to talk about, as she was in the middle of litigating a precedent-setting tax case against the Internal Revenue Service. Silver was a certified public accountant and very knowledgeable. He was able to share information with Rose Marie that strengthened her position in the case, and from his assistance a friendship and trust developed. Her confidence in Silver's abilities was such that she eventually asked him to manage her business and personal financial affairs.

Silver could see that religion was important in Rose Marie's life, and naturally Rose Marie was happy to share her beliefs with him. In response to Silver's interest, Isaac Smoot, who was the president of the Northern States Mission for the Mormon Church, invited him to his home, and together they studied the gospel.[11] When Silver was baptized, Elder LeGrand Richards personally welcomed him into the Church.

Rose Marie later taught Michael Silver's niece Sally, a young Jewish girl searching for answers. Although her own parents were not religious, her grandparents, Max and Ida Silverman, were orthodox Jews. The daily service conducted by her grandfather and the ritual washings conducted by her grandmother were sacred moments in Sally's life. "I once asked my mother about death . . . 'why do people have to die?' My mother pointed to a lampshade and said, 'You see that lampshade? When it gets old, we throw it away, and when people get old, we have to throw them away too.'" Sally continued, "After the episode, I recall pressing my face against the window pane in our living room and looking down from our second-story apartment at all the people on the street. 'I can't die,' I thought over and over again."

From then on, Sally paid particular attention in the synagogue. "I couldn't understand the services, but I remember that one part was a prayer for the dead. Those mourning would rise and chant the prayers accompanied by muffled sobs." At camp one summer, Sally came in contact with a King James Bible. Completely unfamiliar with the New Testament, Sally began reading it for the first time.

"I knew I was reading truth," she said. "What was I to do? I was Jewish, and I believed the New Testament, and that meant believing in Jesus Christ." Sally continued reading and praying in the privacy of her own bedroom. "I was a quiet and obedient little girl, and not at all assertive or troublesome. However, I do know why I chose to tell my parents. To me, it seemed sneaky to have all those new ideas and wonders churning within me and to still keep such an important thing secret from my very own parents." When her parents learned of her beliefs, they ridiculed and scolded her for being stupid. They told her that she was born a Jew and she would die a Jew.

Sally continued her own private form of Christianity in her Jewish home for several years. Uncomfortable with the various churches she investigated, she became despondent and withdrew. She would drive out to the desert in her run-down car to plead with God—"to what kind of a God, I didn't know. For what I pleaded, I didn't exactly know. If there was something out there, I wanted to know what it was."

In her eighteenth year Sally received a phone call from her uncle, Michael Silver. "When you come to California . . . we're going to make you a Mormon," he said. Sally was not impressed.

In June of 1957 Sally had her first lesson from Rose Marie. She had decided to adopt the stance of her philosopher professor and hold that there was no God. But Rose Marie's approach fascinated her. Rose Marie talked about the Jews. "I couldn't believe what I was hearing. She actually was putting into words those vague feelings which had haunted me for the past seven years."

Sally remembered her moment of conversion. She was driving to work one day "singing a song out loud because there was no radio in the Jeep. There was not a thought in my head about religion. Suddenly, I grabbed the steering wheel very tightly. Aloud and with a voice filled with amazement, I said, "It's true! I know it's true!' At that moment, I had a sudden, intense conviction that I would join the Church and that nothing my parents could do, or would do, could stop me."

Later, Sally's brother Harold joined the Church, and Sally married Winston McClare Smith in the Los Angeles Temple. She has served as a seminary teacher, Primary president, Young Women's leader, and as a stake Relief Society president. In a taped interview, she bore her testimony: "My own heart thrills within me as I record these words. I know for myself and of a certainty that Jesus Christ is the Creator of the world and the Redeemer and Savior of all mankind."[12]

Rose Marie also taught Louis Minkin, a Jewish man who sought baptism into the Mormon Church. Interested in the

Mormon religion, Minkin had written to the president of the Church, President David O. McKay, who gave the letter to Elder LeGrand Richards. Elder Richards wrote to Minkin, explaining that he would have Rose Marie Reid contact him. Rose Marie was temporarily living in New York. She met him 15 March 1955 at the Plaza Hotel in New York.

Rose Marie learned that Minkin had been in the army in the Philippines in 1945. He had heard the testimony of a young Mormon man, which had led him to study about the restoration of the gospel. "I swear to you, Sister Reid," Minkin said of that first encounter with the Mormon religion, "the Holy Ghost whispered in my ear, and it was not my mind . . . the meeting could not be a coincidence." His feelings for the gospel matured and grew, and for ten years he had desired to be baptized: "To date I have not been baptized, but I sorely wish I was. My wife however does not yet believe all that I do. She is coming along very nicely though, and I feel sure that in a relatively short time we will both be baptized."[13]

Occasionally some Church member or leader would display some prejudice toward the Jewish people, and both Elder LeGrand Richards and Rose Marie requested that Church leaders make an official statement encouraging its members to be very careful and very accepting of new Jewish members. President David O. McKay, however, responded, "We doubt very much that there is justification for the assumption that there is prejudice to any large extent among our people against the Jewish people."[14]

Following this communication from President McKay, Elder Richards was sent to Los Angeles to give counsel on the Jewish program. He carried with him a message from Henry D. Moyle, one of the Apostles of the Church: "You tell Rose Marie that if she can convert them [the Jewish people] in three lessons, fine. If not, leave them alone."[15]

Elder Richards was obedient, although unhappy. Rose Marie responded with the suggestion that they could work with the younger generation. "It's the parents that we need to take a longer time with," she said. Elder Richards reasoned that if they left the parents out, it would look like Mormons were trying to steal their children away from them. "We wouldn't want to give that impression," he said. His final advice was, "Let's let it wait, just let it wait."[16]

Rose Marie later learned that Elder Moyle's position was that the time for the Jewish people to accept the gospel had not yet come, and that when it did come, the Lord would do the work personally. Although Elder Richards still wanted to see the Jewish work go on, it would now need to be done differently. His heart was with the Jewish work, but he was very careful never to disrupt the unity of the Church's presiding brethren. "I hope you will not feel that I am losing any interest in this work," he said to Rose Marie, but greater emphasis was not possible.[17] His final words must have cut deeply into Rose Marie's heart: "Thank you, Rose Marie, for all you have done and for sending your outlines and visual aid books, and your recordings." The Jewish people would no longer receive special treatment from Mormon missionaries.

Despite the Church's great efforts to take the gospel throughout the world, Elder Richards seemed to be the only General Authority who felt that the Jewish work required a separate, special approach. Daily Rose Marie prayed, "Oh, [he's] got to live forever until this thing gets going again."[18] Although some, including Rose Marie's friend Jan Warner, continued their teaching of Jewish friends, the work as a whole gradually declined.

With a heavy heart, Rose Marie supported this decision from the headquarters of the Church. She recognized that the Church leaders were working very hard and President McKay had just launched a major effort to spread the gospel throughout the world. She was also aware of the extensive programs among the Native Americans in both North and South America. The Jewish work would have its day—this she knew.

Elder Richards' heart was still with the Jewish work. To Rose Marie, he wrote the following:

> In our Quarterly conference of the Quorum of the Twelve, last week, I brought up again the matter of missionary work with the Jewish people and told them how I felt, that we ought to be doing more than we are doing and quoted some of the revelations of the Lord but I rather got sat down on with the thought that we would do the work when the proper time came. I had thought now that Brother Moyle had [died] that probably the

brethren would have a more favorable attitude but that is what I got so I am pretty much hand tied as much as I would like to help promote this work. I have it in my heart. I think the Lord put it there but it is just like He says in Revelations:

"Renounce war and proclaim peace and seek diligently to turn the hearts of children to the fathers and the fathers to the children and again the hearts of the Jews unto the prophets and the hearts of the prophets unto the Jews, lest I come and smite the whole earth with a curse and all flesh be consumed before me."

I do not think the Lord was talking about turning the hearts of the Jews to the dead prophets nor the hearts of the dead prophets unto the Jews, but until authorization comes from above, I suppose it is wise for me to just mark time and do what I can on the side. This, however, does not accord with my feelings and my desires.[19]

Rose Marie was deeply disappointed when the Church discontinued its use of her Jewish lessons. She had spent two years writing the lessons, putting her entire heart and soul into the process despite her feelings of inadequacy. Her experiences had allowed her to understand how Jewish people think, and she understood their strengths and weaknesses. Even though Rose Marie fully supported the Church leaders in their decision, she was brokenhearted to have the work stopped when she felt the Jewish people had been on the verge of so much acceptance.

There is no question that her approach was effective. For every one hundred first lessons taught to Jewish investigators using the traditional lesson plan of the Church, survey results showed that three and one-half persons were baptized. In contrast, with the use of Rose Marie's lessons, from every one hundred first discussions fourteen persons were baptized.

In an unofficial survey conducted among stakes in the Los Angeles area, Rose Marie learned that among the missionaries who used the traditional lessons, Jewish converts came to only five percent. When Rose Marie's discussions were used, the number of converts rose to fifteen percent. Inglewood California Stake had refused to even try her method. The result? "They have not had one [Jewish] baptism," she reported.[20]

Rose Marie left the Jewish work, but it never left her heart. Years later, the Mormon prophet and president, Spencer W. Kimball, would say, "Is it not timely that we begin to preach to Judah as well as the other tribes? . . . There are more Jews in the United States than in all the rest of the world. . . . Should we not now increase our effort to reach them? This does not mean a mission to Jerusalem in these troubled times, but we could begin to reach out for our Jewish brothers just as we do for all others."[21]

The invitation to study and to approach the gospel is always open to all people. However, there exists in the Mormon Church the strong desire to never offend any group of people. The wish not to be approached is always respected by the Mormon Church. Therefore, missionary efforts are made only with the approval and invitation of both governments and peoples alike.

Rose Marie knew in her heart that the time was near when there would be prepared a generation among the Jewish nations that would readily accept the coming of the Messiah. She believed, as the ancient prophets taught, that the gospel would fill the whole earth, that every word the prophets uttered would come to pass, and that one day the tribes of Judah and Joseph would stand side by side to profess the same message—that Jesus is the Christ, and that the Messiah is the Messiah for the whole world.

"Mother always spoke positively of the work," Carole later recalled. "Many times she would say, 'If my lessons converted only one person, it was worth all of the time and effort I put into them. I know that one person led to truth can affect many others, and I always remember the words of the Savior, who said that if you bring one soul unto me, 'how great will be your joy with him in the kingdom of my Father!'" (Doctrine & Covenants 18:15.)

Notes

1. Rose Marie Reid, letter to LeGrand Richards, n.d.
2. *Attention Israel,* n.p., n.d. This pamphlet was privately published by Rose Marie Reid.
3. Rose Marie Reid, Oral History, p. 113.

4. Joseph O. Lie, letter to Rose Marie Reid, 18 January 1959.

5. Mrs. Friedman and Mrs. Dan Rugeti, letter to Rose Marie Reid, n.d.

6. Paul Zimmerman, letter to Rose Marie Reid, n.d.

7. Rose Marie Reid, letter to Marion Heilner, 13 May 1953.

8. Rose Marie Reid, letter to LeGrand Richards, 16 May 1955.

9. Unidentified, undated newspaper clippings in author's possession.

10. Harry Howard to Rose Marie Reid, n.d.

11. Isaac Smoot, letter to Rose Marie Reid, 19 November 1955.

12. Sally Miller Smith, typed interview, n.d.

13. Louis Minkin to Rose Marie Reid, 18 October 1955.

14. First Presidency of the Church (David O. McKay, Stephen L. Richards, J. Reuben Clark), letter to LeGrand Richards, 6 March 1959.

15. Rose Marie Reid, Oral History, p. 132.

16. Ibid.

17. LeGrand Richards, letter to Rose Marie Reid, 25 February 1960.

18. Rose Marie Reid, Oral History, p. 134.

19. LeGrand Richards, letter to Rose Marie Reid, 16 October 1963.

20. Rose Marie Reid, letter to LeGrand Richards, 2 May 1960.

21. Spencer W. Kimball, *Ensign,* May 1975.

22. Rose Marie Reid, Oral History, p.162. See also Revelation 7.

CHAPTER 14

Beauty Inside and Out

In February 1958, a young high school girl who admired the famous swimsuit designer wrote to some friends of Rose Marie, who in turn shared the letter with her. The young girl wrote that her family was poor, her graduation was coming, and she wanted to participate in all the festivities. She was writing to ask that they assist her financially at this special time of her life. It was a delicate situation, but Rose Marie's chief concern was that this young woman be taught correct principles in a loving way.

> Darling [wrote Rose Marie] when I read your letter my heart ached with the memories it brought back to me. Graduation time does cost a lot of money, more than parents can possibly ever be told or it would break their hearts for two reasons. If they had no money to give to you they would feel so badly about it, or if they tried to get the money by a lot of sacrifice they should not make.
> That's why I did not tell my parents that there were senior picnics, senior dances, senior trips, graduation rings, announcements, dresses, dresses, dresses. For they could not afford all those things for me, and they would have been as sad as I was, or more so.
> So I did not send out announcements, and so I

received no graduation presents. I did not go on the trips, I stayed home and worked. I went to one dance, for I had one dress. And a graduation dress that I had made myself. The material had cost a fortune, then about $5.00.

Shall I tell you the story of the lives of the girls who had the money to go to all those things? You can guess, I'm sure. I would not trade places with any one of them, nor with the whole class added together, for I have a far richer life than all of them added together.

I firmly believe that I have it now because I worked harder than all of them. Because there was no one to whom I could go to get money. I had to GROW enough to make it myself. Our Father in Heaven could give it to you if he wanted you to receive it without having to work for it. But he knows how to give his children opportunities. His greatest gift to you and to me is *DESPERATE NEED*.

To have a REAL GENUINE NEED is the greatest incentive in the world. Necessity is the mother of invention. The LASH OF NECESSITY drives people to great things. They would never reach greatness if NEED had not been there forcing them.

So I would not let [my friends] loan you money nor give it to you. That graduation will be gone so soon, but the debt would linger on and before you had it paid you would hate [them] for letting you have it, for you would not have anything to show for it, and you would feel that you were now paying money for nothing.

Yes, there are some times when one must borrow money. One time my whole business would have been lost if I could not have borrowed $290 from my parents. I would not be here now, but for that loan. So I will be indebted to my parents forever for it, and I love them more deeply because that loan meant so much to me, to my children, to my whole future.

But the REASON for borrowing was the ONLY REASON one should ever borrow. For the salvation of life and property. Not for trips, nor clothes. So you just plan to keep your secret and do not make your parents sad because they cannot give you all the luxuries. They are giving you a REASON TO WORK, A REASON TO LIVE, FOR YOU HAVE A REAL *NEED*.

Then you do not borrow because you happen to know some rich people who are in a position with you and your family that they would not dare to say "NO" to you. They want your love and friendship forever. For themselves and for their children. . . .

I love your parents for all the reasons that you know. I hope you understand. There have been a few people in my life who have helped guide me in the right direction when I needed it. I believe I am doing that with you (in doing this for you) right now.

Your memories of this graduation will be happy ones, dear, if you let them be like mine are.

HAPPY GRADUATION, dear, is my wish for you. Not the kind of pleasure that the others will have which will be gone and forgotten, but a secret happiness that will stay with you all your life.

Sincere love,
Rose Marie Reid.[1]

The letter reveals much about Rose Marie—her desire to teach and ensure learning correct principles more than to assure people's comfort, the protective feelings she had for her parents, and the recognition that true wisdom is earned through difficult trials. One understands, too, much of how Rose Marie's environment shaped her, by creating the "desperate need" and "lash of necessity" that drove her to work so hard.

Rose Marie knew of what she spoke. Each phrase is tipped with the silver of experience and the gold of pure love. She believed in the directive to "reprove . . . with sharpness" (Doctrine & Covenants 121:43), afterwards showing forth increased love. This is the power of Rose Marie's teaching philosophy—first, her ability to love deeply, no matter what weakness or offense, and second, the fact that she herself had descended below the experiences of those she taught.

Rose Marie was especially gifted teaching young women. In addition to her own daughters and the young women of her church, she also taught the models and workers at the factories. As she always designed on her models, she had someone read from the Bible, Book of Mormon, or another religious book. Often she would pause to ask the reader to underline specific passages for her. She asked her models and workers how they felt about religion and what they wanted from life.

Said Marion, "The girls loved her . . . She was very much interested in teaching these girls . . . They loved her and loved what she said. She wanted to teach them to improve themselves. . . . She was willing to help them remodel their whole bodies and their faces, whatever needed doing, and she would pay for them to have it done. I don't know how many noses she paid for to be fixed and braces to straighten teeth. She was perfectly willing to do anything to help those girls be more attractive, more eligible, and she meant it in only the cleanest and the best way in the world."

Many models used Rose Marie's teachings to go on to fuller, more vibrant lives. Said one model, Loraine Eiermann, "Rose Marie asked me questions about how I felt about God, the Bible, and life after death. Religion was a comforting subject for me—my mother had died just the year before starting work for Rose Marie Reid . . . [and] I was bitter [as Mother] was not yet 42 years old." Rose Marie would turn the talk to religion as they worked. "It was so natural for her," Loraine continued, "because religion was an around the clock thing in her life. . . . For every question I had, she had a beautiful answer."[2]

Another model, Charlotte Eggers, remembered giving Rose Marie a birthday card that said she was an angel. "She was so touched by this," said Charlotte, "and said how she wished to be an angel. . . .What Rose Marie meant to me is so much more than any experience I can put into words. She always wanted us to be our very best." Charlotte described how Rose Marie would put a "Do not disturb" sign on the door and she would take out her Bible. As they worked, they would read and underline. "[Rose Marie] had so much enthusiasm in [our studies]. . . . She was as excited [as we were] about any new insight we had."[3] Both Charlotte and Loraine were baptized.

"I'll never forget the first fashion show I did for a Rotary Club luncheon," said Charlotte. "The room was filled with men that were ready and waiting to see some models in bathing suits—most having had a drink or two. After ten minutes Rose Marie had changed the whole atmosphere in the room. She had brought them all to a higher level. They were enraptured with her and she was talking about her faith etc. while weaving it around the business. They really lost all interest in us."[4] Charlotte concluded, "I thought of her as mother, friend, spiritual advisor, and angel."

Rose Marie sought not only to improve people's appearance, but also to improve their character. To a group of young women in Los Angeles, she wrote: "All of us know women who ought to be beautiful. . . . Yet there is a hard expression about the otherwise perfect mouth, a suggestion of selfishness about the eyes, of irritation on the fair forehead. . . . The most shadowy hint of an unlovely character will mar the beauty of an otherwise perfect face. . . . Be sure therefore that your character responds charmingly to everything about you, and your face, your voice, and your manner will do likewise. The really beautiful character, the kind that creates an impression of physical loveliness, must in addition to being merely good, be cheerful, tender, refined, and sympathetic. . . . These are the hidden powers."[5]

She taught that if anger were allowed to enter one's heart, it would eventually come to show on the face; that self-consciousness robs a woman of her charm; and that all must learn to be good conversationalists. "When the talk turns to music, art, travel, or baseball, golf, fishing or social activities, and you are unable to find a thing to say, remember, becoming a conversationalist is like becoming anything else, it is a matter of practice. The minute you read or discover something of interest, pass it along."[6]

Rose Marie was especially interested in teaching young Mormon girls to prepare for marriage, that their experiences would not be as painful as her own. "Believe me, girls," she told them, "you are not just competing with the non-Mormon girls, who are very lovely and attractive girls [for the Mormon boys, who, Rose Marie pointed out, could take them to the temple for eternal marriage]. . . . You are competing with Satan, for he knows the power of God. . . . If [Satan] can keep those boys from being effective . . . , he has won the battle. You girls have a double job . . . not only to work out your own salvation but to make certain that every mother's son in this Church never goes with an outside girl. . . . We marry those with whom we associate."[7] As she had worried for her niece Claire marrying a non-Mormon, so she worried for all Mormon girls; Rose Marie knew the great need for marriage partners to be "equally yoked." She also knew that even marriage within the Church could be risky if both spouses did not live the principles of the gospel. She did not want any woman to go through what she had experienced.

Despite her great tact, Rose Marie could speak frankly, although always appropriately. "I want every one of you girls to take your mother and both stand in front of the mirror when you get home," she said to a group of Mormon girls. "If you are not the sweetest, loveliest, most attractive, most beautiful, most darling girl you have ever seen—then you do something about it!" It must have been a startling shock to the young and the naive to realize that the responsibility to be beautiful was no one's but their own. The power was within themselves, and there was no excuse for not being "the most beautiful, most darling girl you have ever seen."[8]

At one conference in Los Angeles, she asked a group of girls in her workshop to smile. She was astonished. "There was something wrong with each girl's teeth!" she said afterward. She asked, "[Do] all the Mormon girls [have] bad teeth? Do they all need orthodontia?" Speaking directly to the parents, Rose Marie said, "The greatest cause of an inferiority complex in your daughter is bad teeth! . . . You have her teeth straightened, whatever it takes to do it." At one time, Rose Marie went so far as to contact the leadership of the Primary (the Mormon organization for children) and ask that they initiate a campaign among the members and local dentists to start providing orthodontic care for all children who came from families who could not afford to pay for the necessary dental care. She even found several dentists who were willing to participate. The Primary was not able to set up such a program, but the organization's general president, La Vern Parmley, encouraged Rose Marie to do all she could.[9] And Rose Marie did, arranging for many children to have their teeth fixed.

A charm course Rose Marie taught at BYU featured lectures on "How never to become angry," "Proper breathing for speaking and voice resonance," "What to say to a boyfriend," "How much do you tell a girlfriend," "Good books for charming women," "Beauty tips," "How to be a proper hostess," "The good conversationalist," and "TEETH!"—Rose Marie's pet personal cause.

After filling out the necessary paperwork in order to teach this class, Rose Marie appended this note: "Writing this letter has taken almost as long as the charm course!" Although she was happy to speak whenever asked, she disliked the trivia and paperwork that accompanied some of her speaking assignments.

During her lifetime, Rose Marie gave well over three hundred great speeches to audiences ranging in size from several hundred to several thousand. On one occasion, she held the rapt attention of more than five thousand people for over two hours on five consecutive nights—a more than remarkable feat. Most amazing is the fact that most of these addresses were given during the 1950s, when she was at her peak in the design world, and therefore, the busiest.

Rose Marie spoke frequently to the youth and the members of her church, partly because the Mormon Church has a lay ministry which relies upon its members to be its teachers and leaders, but also because of her experience and status as the leading women's swimwear designer in the world. Her invitations to speak both to Church members and to other groups are too numerous to mention. But Rose Marie attended and spoke at as many as was humanly possible. To respond to these requests, she often drove or flew hundreds of miles, usually at her own expense.

Like her father before her, Rose Marie had a natural speaking ability, a gift from the early Yanceys, among whom was William Loundes Yancey (1814-1863). A well-known member of the Yancey clan, William practiced law in South Carolina and Alabama. An American Southern Democrat, he introduced his political doctrine, later to become the "Alabama Platform," at the 1848 national Democratic Convention.

Like Rose Marie, William Loundes possessed an unusually charming voice combined with an attractive appearance. This helped him become an effective orator, and from 1848 to 1861 he spoke constantly on Southern rights. He deplored all compromise, and at the 1860 national Democratic Convention he was the acknowledged spokesman for the South. When he finished his

Rose Marie at one of her many speaking engagements

speech and left the convention hall, most of the Southern delegates, all representing states that later seceded from the Union, left with him.

A hand-penciled family note says of William, "His power was himself. How such a great man mounted the rostrum, with what demeanor he endured an interruption, with what gesture he silenced a murmur—such things were remembered and talked about when his reasoning was forgotten." Similarly, people remembered and were inspired by Rose Marie's very presence. Referred to as "the attractive epitome of feminity,"[10] Rose Marie was soft-spoken, with shrewd brown eyes, curly auburn hair, and a dimpled chin. Her shoulders were slightly hunched, a deliberate posture she affected as if to defer to the judgment of others around her.

Rose Marie's patriarchal blessing referred specifically to her speaking ability, saying: "Thou hast a sweet voice. Therefore, wilt thou not use it more? The Lord promises thee that thou shalt save many souls through thy voice; its soft sweet cadence to be trained to tell the story of Mormonism in the most enticing ways, and the burning testimony in thy heart of thy Savior should be born to the Latter-day Saints, and even though thy voice be soft and modest, yet it will be like a two-edged sword which cutteth asunder both joint and marrow. Therefore, do what the Lord asks, for the promise is that your knowledge will be tripled instantly, and the words of your mouth will be fuel to the fires of your soul, and they will kindle fire in the hearts of your listeners. As they pass your tongue they will taste like honey and sounding in people's ears they will be as a harmonious song."[11]

Listening to tapes today, long after the fact, one still senses a breathless excitement, an innate humility, and a lilting tone of endearing love as she spoke. All of these are freshened by insightful wisdom and a practical sense for right and wrong. She possessed the ability to capture any listener. She believed in the fellowship of the whole human family, and she spoke eloquently about it.

Audiences knew that Rose Marie had come from among them as one of very humble means, yet she had risen through hard work and sheer determination against incredible odds to the pedestal of the world. She was a phenomenon—a Mormon woman at the top of the world. She had received the American Sportswear Design Award, being named as the designer who had made the most significant contribution to American sportswear. She had also won the coveted Jenny Award and had been named as Woman of the Year by *The Los Angeles Times*. She was, in fact, the first Mormon woman ever to achieve such international fame—and she had once farmed in an Idaho potato field for the food she ate.

In addition to addressing young Mormon women and local church organizations, Rose Marie taught extension courses for UCLA in 1957 on various topics related to women in professional life; she also taught at BYU Leadership Week. In 1952 she was asked to speak at Brigham Young University where the marketing department was sponsoring a special symposium. The invitation read, "It was with a great deal of pleasure that we learned that 'The Rose Marie Reid' was a member of the L.D.S. Church in good standing. . . . If we could include you in the series of lectures which we are now scheduling for the spring quarter . . . ?"

Her participation was so successful and was received so enthusiastically that she was asked back for the 1953 season. Lockwood Hales, who had been instrumental in getting Rose Marie to attend, received this note of gratitude from the administration: "Thank you for the great contribution you made to the educational and spiritual welfare of 2,000 Brigham Young University students who were assembled this morning in the Field House to hear Rose Marie Reid."[12]

One thank-you note said, "Her story is a tribute to faith and determination in the face of high odds. I was thrilled by her humility and apparent desire to tell us that there is a sure way to success. It was very plain that one cannot divorce the gospel from one's work and still expect the blessings of the Lord."[13] And yet another note described Rose Marie's presentation as "the frosting for the entire course."[14] Similar unsolicited reports came in from over 125 participants.

Rose Marie kept her thoughts in a small stenographer's notebook. As she worked she jotted them down. One entry read: "Such a mixture of emotions accompanies this being a parent—this joy of possessing for our very own the small bundle of humanity, so tiny and helpless and dependent upon us. The feeling of pride that this glorious spirit living in that tiny body chose our home to come to, for such brilliant choice spirits shine thru the eyes of our babies— and then the feeling of humility that makes us want to go on our knees and pray many times a day, 'Oh Father help us to be worthy of these great blessings and give us wisdom.'"[15]

It is not known if this little thought ever made it into a talk, but it certainly reflected some deep thinking at a time in her life that was terribly trying. This poignant thought came during a time when she faced daily bombardments from a husband who wanted no babies, and it reveals both her character and the diligence with which she planned even a Sunday School talk.

During 1953, Rose Marie also participated in the bishopric seminar for the Los Angeles Stake. This would not normally be notable, except that the Los Angeles Stake was then and is still today one of the most influential Mormon bodies in the world. Men like

Rose Marie with Church leaders at the ground breaking
for the Santa Monica Stake Center

LeGrand Richards, John Carmack, John Russon, and Rodney Brady have made the stake a pivotal point in the Mormon Church. Rose Marie also worked with other stakes, including the Pasadena Stake, and grew to know well its president, Howard W. Hunter, who was later to become the president and prophet of the Church.

Her participation amidst this stake's priesthood power marks the level of her influence in the Church. She was eloquent, beautiful, and wise.

In 1954 Rose Marie was again invited to the symposium with the marketing department at BYU. Weldon J. Taylor introduced her by saying, "Going back as far as Plato we find there has been one attribute which is a part of business that has definitely been smiled on by the Gods . . . *beauty*. . . . Sister Reid has devoted her life [to it]." On her way to the meeting, Rose Marie had asked Weldon "how much religion" she should put into this talk? Because, she said, "if I tell the truth it will be *all religion*." And she meant it.

In 1959, she addressed the entire student body of BYU. Then, as she had earlier, she described how Dean Olson had said, "I want to tell every Mormon to go around and say to his friends 'I am a Mormon' because the most amazing and the most exciting things happen. You find so many people who will say, 'Is there a Mormon

Church here? I would like to go.' And you say, 'Yes, indeed it is that Church of Jesus Christ of Latter-day Saints that you see up there on the corner.' And they say, 'Why, I pass that every day. That is not Mormon, is it?' Please could we, in parentheses, under the sign 'Church of Jesus Christ of Latter-day Saints,' put the word 'Mormon'?"[16] This was the first time such a suggestion was ever made.

Rose Marie's speech was published and distributed in bundles by the thousands. The American Association of University Women asked her to address them in Ventura, California, and the president of the BYU faculty wives association, Sarah M. Grow, wrote to Rose Marie inviting her to speak to that group. Previous speakers had included Lavina Fugal, American Mother of the Year; Juanita Brooks, outstanding Utah author and historian; and Florence Jepperson Madsen, a famous composer and conductor.

Rose Marie was also asked to speak to the wives of the General Authorities of the Church. Norma Anderson, wife of Joseph Anderson, wrote to Rose Marie: "Information has come to me that on different occasions when you have received distinct honors in the business world, you have attributed your success as a speaker to the opportunities and experiences you have had to participate in various church activities."[17]

Rose Marie was also a popular speaker among other groups. She was invited to be the featured speaker at the Religious Emphasis Week at the Woodbury College in Los Angeles, sponsored by the Christian Science campus organization, the Newman Club, the Philologus Club, and Lamba Delta Sigma. Rose Marie was honored to share the week-long program with Paul H. Dunn, who would become an extremely popular and influential Mormon author and speaker.

That same year, Elder LeGrand Richards wrote, "Just a line to tell you that I have seen the announcement in the *California Intermountain News* of the five-week course to be presented by Brigham Young University in the Brentwood Ward recreation hall entitled, 'Charming You,' and you are to be the teacher. I don't know who could be chosen who could do a better job and I commend you for it."[18] The course was so successful that Rose Marie was put on the speakers circuit for all BYU off-campus courses.

Numerous church talks in Southern California also kept Rose Marie busy. Donna Haueter of the Westdale Ward wrote: "I gained so much from [your talk] that I just had to send you this little note of appreciation. . . . I have many more boyfriends since I have learned to wear appropriate clothes and put make-up on correctly."[19] Donna's letter helps us see that even in church meetings and firesides, Rose Marie Reid could not resist changing people physically as well as spiritually.

Notes

1. Rose Marie Reid, letter written to a young girl, 4 April 1958 (San Francisco). The name of the young girl to whom Rose Marie wrote this letter is not given in order to respect her privacy.
2. Loraine Eierman, letter to Carole Reid Burr, 4 September 1988.
3. Charlotte Eggers, letter to Carole Reid Burr, n.d.
4. Ibid.
5. Rose Marie Reid, typed manuscript of speech, n.d.
6. Rose Marie Reid, personal file notes, n.d.
7. Rose Marie Reid, address at Southern California Leadership Week, August 1959.
8. Ibid.
9. Letter, LaVern Parmley to Rose Marie Reid, 13 November 1957
10. Hammond, "Miss Reid Suits Swimmer Best," *Los Angeles Times*.
11. Rose Marie Reid, Patriarchial Blessing.
12. Wayne B. Hales, letter to Lockwood Hales 1 June 1953 (Provo, Utah).
13. Ibid.
14. Weldon J. Taylor, note to Marketing Department, 5 June 1953.
15. Rose Marie Reid, personal file notes, n.d.
16. Rose Marie Reid, speeches given at Brigham Young University, Provo, Utah, 1 June 1953 and 18 May 1959.
17. Norma Anderson, letter to Rose Marie Reid, 15 May (no year).
18. LeGrand Richards, letter to Rose Marie Reid, 12 July 1957 (Salt Lake City, Utah).
19. Donna Haueter, letter to Rose Marie Reid, 20 November 1957 (Westdale, California).

*World tour in 1959 with (left to right) Ned Redding,
Sharon, Rose Marie, Bishop William Jackson*

CHAPTER 15

Europe

From time to time, Rose Marie's children would ask her, "Mother, how much money do you make? Five thousand dollars or a million?" But it didn't make that much difference to Rose Marie or her children as long as their needs were met. Her success was entirely in the Lord's hands. Rose Marie always felt that the Lord guided every step of her life. In her oral history she said, "If I write [my story] all I'll say is the Lord did this and the Lord did that."[1]

In 1958 her sales figures had topped $14 million. (According to the *U.S. Consumer Index* for 1958, [factoring X 4.52] this would be comparable to $63.5 million gross revenue in 1990.) In 1959 she was selling in 46 countries, and she had been the largest manufacturer of women's swimsuits in the world since 1954.

To promote her international image, Rose Marie traveled to Europe twice during the 1950s. The Kesslers and others encouraged her to see the fashion centers of the world. They were also afraid that somehow the source of her inspiration would run dry or the charm that created the magic would somehow come to an end, so they decided to send her abroad for more inspiration. She resisted taking the time at first, but new sales forces were operating in Switzerland, England, Holland, West Germany, and Milan with Dusseldorf, Amsterdam, and Brussels under consideration as potential areas for expansion. Rose Marie understood that the European markets were important, and she consented to the trip.

Everywhere Rose Marie traveled, the red carpet was laid out for her. The Marquis MacSwiney of Mashanaglass wrote: "I am at your disposal, and if there is anything that I can do to assist you during your stay in London, and if it is in my power to do it, I will be only too pleased to help."[2]

Upon deplaning in London, Rose Marie was met by journalists from seven newspapers who interviewed her for four hours, after which a chauffeur escorted her through the city.

On tour in Milano, she met a young guide named Julia, who was so impressed with Rose Marie's ability to convey genuine love that she wrote a parting note as Rose Marie left for Paris: "I saw your areoplane leaving and it was very sad for me, thinking that perhaps a long time will pass before we meet again. . . . I felt immediately a great affection and I will always remember how pleasant it has been for me to show you this little bit of my country."[3] Almost no one left Rose Marie's presence without feeling this love.

As Rose Marie traveled from Italy to Switzerland, she glanced through a newspaper. To her complete astonishment, she came across her name. "I was so surprised to be reading the paper on the way to Switzerland, and find my own name jumping out at me," she wrote to Marion. "This newspaper is the most widely read in Europe. Ann Scott James is the fashion Bible, according to my little guide. . . . I had met her, and had dinner with Emilio [de Pucci], who introduced us: 'Rose Marie, this is Ann.'" Emilio had described Ann to Rose Marie as "the highest paid journalist in Europe." After starting with *Harpers*, Ann had become head of *Vogue* in Europe before the *Sunday Express* had hired her away from them. Said Emilio to Rose Marie, "[Ann] writes one page a week, and it sells the whole paper."

Apparently Emilio had brought swimsuits for his office staff when he returned from Los Angeles. Ann had tried one on and kept it. "[Ann] told me she had never liked a swimsuit before in her life," Rose Marie said. "How did I make them so different? I answered, but did not dream it was for publication! It was so thrilling, really, to find it so by accident."[4]

The article was captioned "Bright Ideas for the Beach" and Ann wrote, "I met a woman this week who is the world's top designer of swimsuits—Rose Marie Reid of California. In just seven years she has built up a women's swimsuit business which is the biggest and best in America. She gave me some ideas that I would like to shout from the housetops." After quoting Rose Marie's philosophy on solving all the different figure problems, Ann concluded, "Rose Marie Reid is a remarkable woman as well as a clever designer. She is a Mormon, does not drink or smoke . . . knows the Bible by heart . . . works fanatically, often far into the night."[5]

The article was some consolation to her, Rose Marie confided to Marion, when she discovered that Switzerland was "closed," and she could not buy any of the watches at half-price "that everyone else who comes to Europe seems to be able to do. All I could do was eat divine Swiss pastry and look at more lakes and mountains and castles perched on highest peaks. That I will never understand. Wherever there is an inaccessible peak, someone has built a castle there. . . . There is a cable car to one which is a restaurant, and lights up one mountain top at night."[6]

She continued, "I find one can take only a certain amount of sightseeing at a time, and then it is like overeating." Exhausted, she commented, "My head really will not contain much more." As she left Paris, she said, "I feel awfully selfish. I bought only for myself! I lack the gift [of choosing] completely! . . . Mrs. Hussey brought me back a lipstick case from Paris."[7]

During one of Rose Marie's trips to Europe, she made a particular point of taking Carole to the French Riviera. She wanted to show her daughter something that she knew would never come to America. "It was the bikini," said Carole. "She told me that American women had too much moral fiber to allow it." But her mother was wrong.

Rose Marie's disgust with the bikini was well known throughout the swimsuit industry and was amply illustrated by her comments to the press. "The man who designed the bikini," she said, "thinks just because he can wear a topless bathing suit, that . . . girls can too."[8] One Idaho mother wrote to her expressing thanks for her strong stand against the bikini: "My son asked me . . . to get your opinion of the topless bathing suit. . . . I told him I knew how you felt about them just from what you said about the bikini. . . . When

*Rose Marie Reid receiving the most prestigious award in fashion, the 1958
American Designer Sportwear Award at the St. Regis Hotel, New York City*

a mother is trying to teach her children modesty, answers to these
questions are very important."[9]

To Steve Hale of the *Deseret News*, she said, "The bikini is
hideous, vulgar, and immoral." *Time* magazine also carried a short
brief on Rose Marie's feelings: "Bikinis, to hear the designers tell it,
are favorably regarded only by the well-shaped women who buy
them. 'Most manufacturers do not like bikinis,' admits Rose Marie
Reid, one of the most popular of the U.S. swimsuit stylists. 'They
are vulgar, hideous, immoral.' Fred Cole of Cole of California
agrees."[10] Similar accounts were carried by the *Miami News*.[11] The
Arizona Republic carried Rose Marie's picture with the caption: "No
Bikinis for This Lady of Fashion."[12]

Rose Marie's elegant yet practical approach toward swimsuit

design attracted numerous awards, the most prestigious of which was the American Sportswear and Design Award, sponsored by *Sports Illustrated*, in 1958. (In the world of fashion, this award is equal to the Oscar in filmmaking). Rose Marie shared the "Sporting Look of the Year" award with Bonnie Cashin.[13] The award was presented to "the designer of women's sportswear who has shown the greatest inventiveness and creativeness . . ., who has established distinctive new areas of design in the women's sportswear field."[14]

Telegrams and letters poured in. One fashion editor of a well-known and respected magazine wrote that it was "just what we expected of you and most deservedly so."[15] Helen Delbar of Everglaze; Dolly Reed of Max Factor cosmetic company; Phil Altbaum, famous dressmaker; Lynn Norby of *Harper's Bazaar*; and Edward Donnelly of John Donnelly & Sons; along with a hundred others—all sent similar congratulations.

Marjorie Griswald, who had recognized Rose Marie's talent and genius from their first meeting, joined in the tribute: "I think back to the first time [she] came into the office, and I realize what 'big oaks from little acorns grow.' [Her] life has been a miracle. Rose Marie [is] one of the true stories that is more exciting than fiction."[16]

Rose Marie's competition for the award had been formidable. Twenty-four nationally known designers were nominated, five from California: Rose Marie Reid, Margit Fellegi of Cole, Jane Ford of Sportsmaster, John Weitz with Elon of California, and Mary Blair of White Stagg. (It is interesting to note that Ms. Blair was nominated while working for the Tabak Corporation; Louis Tabak had originally warned Jack Kessler that there was no market for Rose Marie's designs.)

Rose Marie Reid and Bonnie Cashin's selection marked the first time the awards had been swept by women alone. The awards committee included the most prestigious figures in the world of fashion, from the president of Macy's of New York City and the president of I. Magnin Co. in California, to the president of Neiman-Marcus, Inc., in Dallas, and the fashion editor of the *New York Times*.

The award was an advertising bonanza worth hundreds of thousands of dollars in publicity since it resulted from the ballots of six hundred retail executives across the nation. Elena Montville of *Sports Illustrated* immediately telegrammed the company to get "glossy photos" for all lines to the east coast, and Rose Marie flew east for the dinner and awards ceremony on 28 May 1956. The presentations were made at the St. Regis Hotel, where one hundred top stores in the country were represented alongside the industry leaders.

The tie between Cashin and Rose Marie created a small stir because of its unexpectedness. The auditing firm of Ernst and Ernst, which tabulated the votes, had not announced the results prior to the awards ceremony, so a duplicate trophy had to be made for Bonnie Cashin. The trophy created especially for this award was designed by Bruce Gilchrist and created by Sidney Smith, a well-known sculptor. It featured a design mannequin of gold wire surrounded by gilded laurel branches.

Nearly every newspaper across the country carried the awards announcement. Idaho, of course, was quick to claim Rose Marie as a native, as were Los Angeles and Vancouver. In each city, newspapers featured the facts of her sojourn in their state. The *Idaho Statesman* reported: "Ex-Idahoan Rose Marie Reid Wins N.Y. Designer's Award."[17] The *Los Angeles Examiner* captioned their article, "Everything's Coming up Roses."

Rose Marie Reid, Inc., stock on the open market immediately took a jump with the announcement of the award, and the California company declared a larger-than-usual dividend for the quarter.

Rose Marie began making appearances on national talk shows. She was a guest on the Mike Douglas show, and interviewed with Dee Parker of KABC. She also rejected an offer to be the guest on George Burns' show. Rose Marie's swimsuits were one of the daily prizes presented on NBC's popular program, *Queen for a Day*, hosted by Jack Bailey.

With the award, Rose Marie entered the designers' hall of fame, but she always shared the credit with others—her design department, pattern makers, seamstresses, management, marketing, and her family. "I didn't do anything that special," she'd say. Yet how far the little Weiser, Idaho, girl had come! When she walked down the boardwalk carrying that bag of one hundred silver dollars, few could have guessed how her beauty, talent, and effort would pay off in achieving the highest recognition in her field.

Rose Marie was also selected by *The Los Angeles Times* in 1955 as one of their Ten Women of the Year. Her co-honorees were

*KSL appearance with Arch Madsen, President of
KSL-TV and Jacki Nokes in Salt Lake City.*

Louise Brough, tennis celebrity; Dorothy Kirsten, opera star; Mrs. Henry Salvatori, civic leader; Hedda Hopper, newspaper personality; Mrs. Nelbert M. Chouinard, art educator; Ruth Shellhorn, landscape architect; Marion Pike, artist; Sister Frederica, social worker; and Dr. Ruth Alice Boak, medical researcher. Each woman was a force in her chosen field; to be included as part of the group was a notable achievement.

It was in the *Times* article that Fay Hammond, writing about Rose Marie, said: "Rose Marie is a permanent 32 years old, but she could make it an even 30 without lopping off birthdays."[18]

Of all the honors Rose Marie received, the one that she loved the most was the hybrid rose created in her honor by Milton L. Whisler, floriculturist and head of Germain's California Research Department. Whisler was inspired by the lovely mixture of colors he saw in Rose Marie's 1955 swimsuit line. He wanted to honor her name, so he refined a long-stemmed rose with beautifully formed buds that opened to "dawn pink, set off by deep green foliage," suggestive of evergreen leaves.[19]

The Rose Marie Reid Rose stood at the juncture of an illustri-

Roses were her trademark.

ous and renowned line. Its two parent roses were the Queen Elizabeth Rose, an All American Award winner in 1955 and the holder of numerous English awards, and the widely heralded Chrysler Imperial Rose, 1953 All-American winner. The Rose Marie was a tea rose that measured six inches across and often doubled, giving it beautiful lasting quality.

Another unexpected honor came to Rose Marie when she and her accountant, Michael Silver, took a break from their financial meetings to have lunch in nearby Brentwood Village. By chance, the Brentwood city officials and the Chamber of Commerce were having a luncheon meeting at the same restaurant. Rose Marie overheard their discussion regarding the lack of funds to repave the village roads and maintain the parking lots in the village. She and Silver had just been discussing her need for some tax-deductible donations for the year. To everyone's surprise, she walked over to their table and donated enough money to the village to repave the roads. She earned the name of "village financial angel," and a few months later she was notified that she had been awarded the title of honorary mayor of Brentwood.

Far greater than the pride she felt upon receipt of these awards was Rose Marie's pride in her first grandchild. Her daughter Carole had married James B. Burr in 1958. The next year Rose Marie's only son, Bruce, married Marie Foutz on 12 June 1959. One day later, Carole gave birth to her first son and Rose Marie's first grandson, Bryan James Burr.

Rose Marie's long time friend and business associate, Lou Tabak, wrote her a letter of congratulations. "You are entering a brand new life, with a new interest that will fascinate you," he said, and added, "The fact that the baby weighed 9 pounds 13 ounces is symbolic of the mass production of the Rose Marie Reid enterprises, as well as the quality of these enterprises."[20]

Notes

1. Rose Marie Reid, Oral History, p. 57.
2. Rose Marie Reid, letter to Marion Heilner, 3 November 1959 (Athens, Greece).
3. Julia [no last name], letter to Rose Marie Reid, 8 November 1956 (Milan, Italy).
4. Rose Marie Reid, letter to Marion Heilner, n.d. (Milan, Italy).
5. Ibid.
6. Ibid.
7. Rose Marie Reid, letter to Marion Heilner, n.d.
8. *Viking Scroll* (Ricks College student newspaper), 15 December 1964.
9. Mrs. Irven Christensen, letter to Rose Marie Reid, n.d.
10. *Time*, 16 May 1960, n.p.
11. *Miami News*, 28 January 1959, p. 4B.
12. *Arizona Republic*, 9 June 1964, p. 20
13. *Utah Peace Officer*, June 1959, p. 9.
14. Ibid.
15. Arden Roney, letter to Rose Marie Reid, 6 June 1958.
16. Marjorie Griswald, letter to Rose Marie Reid, n.d.
17. *Idaho Statesman*, 31 May 1958.
18. Hammond, "Miss Reid Suits Swimmer Best," *Los Angeles Times*.
19. Bea Jones, garden editor, quoted in "The Story of the Rose Marie Reid Rose," publicity brochure printed by the Rose Marie Reid Company, n.d.
20. Lou Tabak, letter to Rose Marie Reid, 24 June 1959.

CHAPTER 16

Years of Blessings, Years
of Tragedy

For Rose Marie, the fifties had been years of triumph. In stark contrast, the sixties would be years of trial and hardship for the Rose Marie Reid family.

When Rose Marie had finished writing her Jewish missionary lessons, she penned a little note: "The Lord must really want these lessons written because it hasn't wrecked my health staying up so late nights."[1] Tragically, however, not long after, she was rushed to the hospital, her body exhausted and her strength gone. At the family's insistence, she went to the Mayo Clinic. There she had a complete physical and was released with a clean bill of health.

Only one week after her release from the clinic, Helen King found Rose Marie lying on the floor of her home, bleeding internally from an ulcer. Again she was rushed to the hospital, this time for immediate surgery; three-quarters of her stomach was removed. Already near death, Rose Marie experienced an especially slow recovery because the operating surgeon had left a sponge inside the surgical site, causing a virulent infection throughout her body. A second surgery was performed to remove the sponge and drain the infection.

Carole, who was living in Provo, hurried to her mother's side.

She had originally planned to spend only a week or so with her, but due to complications from the surgery, Carole stayed several months.

While in the hospital, Rose Marie received hundreds of bouquets of beautiful flowers—so many that she had them sent throughout the hospital, where they filled nearly every patient's room. Hundreds of letters arrived to encourage her. Many asked about her missionary work: "How have you possibly accomplished all you have done?" asked one well-wisher. Requests continued to pour in for her missionary lessons.

Later, Carole would admit that she was stunned when she saw her mother, pale and weak, lying in her hospital room. Her mother had always seemed invincible, energetic, courageous. That her mother, always so strong, could appear so vulnerable frightened Carole.

Carole was not the only one frightened by Rose Marie's vulnerability. Jack and Nina Kessler, as well as Paul Haberfeld, the new general manager whom they had hired, began to worry that they had placed all their eggs in one basket. Should something happen to Rose Marie, they would be completely lost. Jack and Nina no longer wanted to be so heavily involved in the day-to-day decisions; they wanted to retire and enjoy the fruits of their labors. To protect themselves, the Kesslers and Haberfeld brought in additional designers, including some that Rose Marie herself had taught.

With the structure of the company greatly altered, a politics and competition were introduced into the company that had not been there previously. Rose Marie was frustrated by the many additional steps necessary to appease the design committee. Now all the designers were expected to present their designs in front of the group to make their designs a team effort. All designers were expected to comment and share in the process. Rose Marie's designs were no exception from this process.

Because of Rose Marie's innate sense of proportion and design, her suits were flawless; the other designers, many young and inexperienced, felt that it was nevertheless their responsibility to participate in the process. They often suggested changes that did not serve to improve the design. This meant lengthy delays, which was frustrating to Rose Marie.

She understood, however, that when responsibility is shared, it is important to allow everyone to contribute. Her approach to this problem was to take a completed suit and add something extraneous so that the other designers could comment on it and feel they had added their opinion. One time she deliberately placed a large rose on a completed suit. The designers said, "Take off the rose," and so she did. The suit was then exactly as she had planned.

An additional problem Rose Marie encountered was that while she would continue to receive a royalty for suits that bore her name, now some of the suits bearing her name were not her designs. And while Rose Marie remained adamant against production of the bikini, the others did not feel as strongly as she did. While the Kesslers had frequently listened to Rose Marie's counsel and even paid tithing to their religious organization, Paul Haberfeld especially was extremely threatened by Rose Marie and by her God. "Do you have to bring your religion in every time you give speeches?" was Haberfeld's recurrent criticism.

When Paul Haberfeld and the Kesslers decided to expand the company into Van Nuys, California, it was a serious miscalculation. In spite of the new plant's beautiful design, it was located in an area out of the mainstream of the manufacturing district. The skilled workers the company had formerly employed near the L. A. airport would not venture across the Sepulveda Pass into the San Fernando Valley. Consequently, training had to begin again from the very bottom up.

On the new factory, Rose Marie wrote her friend Helen King, "Maybe you have heard from L. A. that Rose Marie Reid, Inc., is building a big new factory in San Fernando Valley. I guess with freeways, it won't be any further from home than now, but the convenience to the airport meant a lot to me. It was being quietly discussed before I left, but I didn't think they'd move so soon, so I said nothing. Since we built the last building we have grown more than ten times in volume, but only double in space, so that's why. I hate change though! So I feel like running when I think of all the problems it presents. . . ."[2]

The company also lost nearly an entire year's profits because of one major fabric buyer's poor quality control. The faulty fabric was a "beautiful, expensive" material, but it could not be sewn without leaving needle holes, and most of it came back for refunds.

Rose Marie Reid finally decided to leave the company, accepting the settlement of fifty thousand dollars a year for five years. Of this arrangement, she said later, "It was a blackmail deal to me. 'Either give up your contract so we can deal or we go into bankruptcy and your name will be sold to the highest bidder, to be used on a prostitute home, if they buy it,'" wrote Rose Marie to Helen.[3]

Rose asked Helen to keep this information confidential and added, "What I am telling others is also what you must say. All businesses are merging. Cole and Catalina are both Keysor Roth now. White Stagg has been combined with us years ago for mutual advantage sales wise, and now production is combining also. It's a good way to get capital gain out of the business, and yet retain stock. I retired last year, [and] I know Jack and Nina envied me, and want to retire. With White Stagg they can retire too. So it has worked out well for everybody.

"That's our story, my dear. But I hope someday I get a chance to say to Nina, 'What price bikinis now, Nina?' For the Lord's blessings stopped when they were started, and no matter how they tried they could get nowhere without the Lord."

Rose Marie always felt it was their insistence on making the bikini that led to the company's ultimate demise. She believed that the Lord was responsible for the success of her company—and she also believed that God allowed the fall of the company when it no longer protected the women who were to wear its product.[4]

Between 1957 and 1960, net sales at Rose Marie International had increased from $13.5 million to $18.1 million. Between 1957 and 1961, stock appreciated from 6 7/8 to 18 3/4. However, by 1962, stock had fallen to a low of 4 1/12. A potential $28 million for 1966 had been projected, and on 23 May 1962, "the company paid its 22nd consecutive quarterly dividend. . . , completing a 5 1/2-year unbroken dividend record."[5] It was the last dividend the company ever paid.

The following year, in 1963, after Rose Marie left the company, Jack Kessler could not pay off his loans, and he told Harry Cohen to try to get a merger with White Stagg. Previously, White Stagg had asked for a merger but their offer had been rejected. White Stagg sales people had been used early on to market Rose Marie

Reid swimsuits, but the business became so large that White Stagg had asked their sales people to choose which company they preferred to represent. Most of them chose Rose Marie Reid.

This was naturally very hard for the White Stagg company, a difficulty that was compounded when White Stagg asked for a merger. They were poorly treated by the Kesslers, Haberfeld, and Cohen who, the White Stagg officials felt, had "insulted" them.

Jack Kessler fired Paul Haberfeld, then attempted a merger with White Stagg, who was never able to pick up the offer. Munsingwear acquired the company, but when they began to manufacture bikinis, Rose Marie immediately brought legal action to regain her name.[6] Two years later, they were forced to close their doors and lay off all personnel.

By 1965, all American swimsuit manufacturers were making the bikini by the thousands. In fact, Cole had to jump to keep up with bikini demands, having underestimated the market by some 200,000 units. They created three "scandal" designs that year—the "Savage," the "Outrageous," and the "Showdown."

Mildred Goldman, sportswear buyer for Saks Fifth Avenue, formerly one of Rose Marie Reid's best fashion markets, called bikini sales "fantastic." "Several women over 60 bought Scandals," she said, "and I had to tell some size 20s who demanded one that, great as it was, it just wasn't for them."[7]

Rose Marie, however, would never make bikinis, and her company, even after several attempts to revive its financial condition, never successfully produced bikinis. Her name would continue to grace many other products, including swimsuits that she did not design, but she personally would not make bikinis. She felt that it was as though God himself had declared a line beyond which His help would not go.

To friends and associates, Rose Marie did not reveal the entire story behind her decision to leave the Rose Marie Reid company. Instead, she told them that her decision was because her mother's health was getting worse and she needed to care for her.

For Mothers' Day in 1961, Bruce, his wife Marie, and their daughter, Allene Reid, traveled from their home in Provo to Los Angeles, planning to spend the day with Rose Marie. Marie was

Marie and Bruce Reid with baby daughter Allene

expecting a second child and Rose Marie was fitting her with maternity clothes, while the housekeeper, Josephine, they thought, was watching little Allene. It is a mystery to everyone how such a small child—just one year and one day—was able to find her way out the door of the house, across the large driveway and parking area and the extensive grounds, past the rose garden to the swimming pool. Barely learning to walk, Allene nevertheless made her way to the pool and tumbled into it. When it was realized that she was missing, everyone began searching. It was Rose Marie's secretary, Jan Warner, who found Allene in the pool, floating face down. Bruce tried desperately to revive his little daughter, but she died in his arms.

Rose Marie anguished over the pain that Bruce and Marie suffered at the death of their baby. Their loss was made even more painful by the extensive coverage that appeared repeatedly in the media because Rose Marie was so well known.

Not long after, Bruce and Marie moved into the Brentwood mansion. Bruce was working on several projects, including the prototype for a hydrofoil boat, a check guarantee card, and the company which would become the R & M Living Wig.

When Marie gave birth to their second child, Rose Marie

watched with a breaking heart as Bruce, who had so lovingly cared for his small daughter during her short life, now distanced himself from his son, Spencer, "as if he refused to be hurt again," said his sister Carole. Jan Warner also noted Bruce's detachment, and so, she said, "Spencer became mine. I would hold him in the sewing room, and he'd look up at the ceiling." But as they sat together, Jan was overcome with a strange feeling—"as if the angels would shortly come for him," she told Rose Marie.

In 1963, Jan saw the fulfillment of her early premonitions. While Bruce and Marie were living in Rose Marie's home, little Spencer, at barely two and a half years old, also crossed the driveway and the rose garden, and fell into the swimming pool as his sister had before him. Although Spencer had been schooled in infant swimming and could swim the full length of the pool, that particular day he was wearing heavy corrective shoes. The added weight and awkwardness of the shoes were too much for his young muscles.

His mother was rehearsing for a church program in the living room when she suddenly saw that Spencer was missing. Quickly looking around her, she ran at last to the pool, where she found him. Only two weeks previously she had had a dream in which she had found her son in the pool, in exactly the setting she now found him.

When the media heard of this second tragedy, there was a great deal of speculation. How could this have happened a second time? they asked. Where had the parents been? How could they have allowed this to happen? Rose Marie's guilt compounded her grief.

On the very day of Spencer's death, Marie's mother, Pauline Foutz, was in the Los Angeles Temple. To her surprise, she saw Spencer standing in the temple dressed in white. At that time, still unaware of his death, she was completely puzzled as to why he was there. Bruce and Marie, however, could not be comforted.

Although the stake patriarch, Charles Norberg, gave Bruce a blessing of comfort, attempting to alleviate some of his tremendous pain, Bruce would never be the same man again. Nor would his wife, Marie, shattered at the death of her second child, ever be the same again.

In the wake of these enormous tragedies, the mansion that Rose Marie had bought with such joy was never again a lovely place for the family. In 1965 Rose Marie sold the property; the house was torn down and divided into eight lots. Gone were the lovely rose gardens, the swimming pool, the stables and orchards—all gone. In their place today stands Rose Marie Lane. Eight lovely homes line the street where children still laugh and play, from time to time remembering with awe the haunting legend of the drowned children. According to Bill Balon, who lives almost exactly where the mansion once stood, the children imagine they can hear the cries of the two babies. "They have made it into a tragic legend," he said.[8]

Mormon doctrine teaches that children who die before the age of eight, which is the age of accountability, go to the highest kingdom of heaven (Doctrine & Covenants 137:10). The mission of little children who die so young, Mormons are taught, is simply to come to earth, receive a body, and go on to another assignment. They are too pure and perfect to remain on the earth to be tested. Said Carole, "Although Mother understood this doctrine of life and death, she simply could not look at the pool and not feel the pain." Despite the happiness that so many had shared with her at her home and on the surrounding grounds, "she simply could not remain there with the memories."

Some time later, Rose Marie moved her mother, Marie, and her Aunt Florence to Utah. She promised to build them a home with a view of the beautiful Wasatch Mountains. Because Jonathan Logan, a prestigious apparel company, had expressed a desire to license her name and to continue manufacturing swimsuits bearing her label, she still traveled frequently to New York. She agreed to teach them the magic of her fit and designs. Despite her poor health, Rose Marie stayed in New York for six months, working with Mr. David Schwartz, president of the company and a businessman she highly respected.

In 1965, on 13 July, Rose Marie's youngest brother, Don, died. He had suffered with poor health his entire life and had died while still relatively young.

Marie's health continued to be very poor and Rose Marie wrote to Helen King, "Mother improves one day and then has two bad ones. She hardly eats at all, and weighs 116 this morning. I cannot understand why the improvement is not constant. I guess it's emotion. . . . The day she thought Aunt Florence was coming she walked a lot, but when I phoned and found she was not coming, she couldn't even pull herself out of the chair, and could hardly walk with me practically lifting her."[9] Marie's skin was so tender that the slightest touch caused her pain.

On 8 September 1965, *Women's Wear Daily* reported that the Rose Marie Reid Company had "nothing left but a name." The company's report to stockholders revealed that it had no funds, no inventory, no employees, no takers, and no plans to continue production. Although they had paid all their creditors, they were now closing their doors. The letter, signed by C. Morgan Aldrich, Jr., noted that Rose Marie Reid had been unable to make "satisfactory arrangements" with anyone to take over operations. There were no interested parties at that time.[10]

Rose Marie felt deeply responsible for the stockholders, who, because of their confidence in her, had purchased stock as an investment for their future. Many contacted her, distressed over their investment. Even though Rose Marie knew the stock was worthless, she could not bear to have them lose their life's investment, so she bought their stock. "All this, when her own financial future was in doubt," said Sharon.

On 11 October 1965, Rose Marie's mother also died just three months after the death of her youngest son. She had been Rose Marie's closest companion from the fruit farms of Idaho to the factories of Los Angeles.

Rose Marie felt a loneliness as never before. She had always revered her mother and father, giving them the credit for her talents and her faith in God. Her only consolation was her sure knowledge that after twenty-seven years of separation, Marie and Elvie were together as they had been in their youth.

Tragedy continued to stalk her when, in July 1966, Rose Marie's brother, Hugh, and his wife, Elinor, were tragically killed in an airplane crash over the Pacific Ocean. They had been entertaining the U.S. troops abroad with his landscape paintings. The weather had been stormy, and the plane had crashed while attempting to land off the coast of Alaska. All aboard had been lost at sea. Hugh had been a kind and loving substitute father to Rose Marie's children, as well as a steadfast support to her.

The ultimate tragedy for Rose Marie would be Bruce's decision to reject the teachings of the Church. Almost ten years after the death of his two oldest children, Bruce and his wife and children would move to Europe and the Mid-East, adopting the 1960s free-thinking philosophies.

Rose Marie had invested most of her remaining monies in Bruce's business ventures, always hoping that his genius, which she felt far surpassed her own, would bring him recognition and some compensation for his troubled childhood and tragic losses. She preferred to view his departure as a search for peace, and she never ceased praying that he would discover the peace that she knew, born also from suffering. "We hoped she would live to see the blessing in this tragedy," said Carole, but she consoled herself with Rose Marie's words: "I have to remember he is Heavenly Father's son first—and then mine."

"All of our lives," said Sharon, "we heard Mother say, 'Tragedies turn into blessings. All you have to do is wait a little while and look back and you will see it is true. No matter how hard things may get, in time you will see purpose for every experience in your life. The most important benefit in a tragedy is that you seek to know God and He is always near. Soon everything plays together like a beautiful concert, and you recognize the Lord's hand in every moment of your life.'"

Notes

1. Handwritten note in Rose Marie Reid's personal files, n.d.
2. Rose Marie Reid, letter to Helen King, 4 August 1963.
3. Ibid.
4. Gwen Tanner, *Sun and Valley Reporter*, San Fernando, California, 18 September 1958.
5. Will Lane, "What Happened to Rose Marie Reid?" *Western Advertising*, September 1966, pp. 54, 58.
6. *Women's Wear Daily*, 8 September 1965, p. 24.
7. Mildred Goldman, quoted in *The Wall Street Journal*, 10 July 1965, p. 1.
8. Bill Balon, interview, 1 March 1990.
9. Rose Marie Reid, letter to Helen King, 4 August 1963.
10. *Women's Wear Daily*, p. 24.

CHAPTER 17

Endless Lawsuits

At the same time that Rose Marie was facing distress in so many areas of her life, her friend and financial advisor, Michael Silver, was resisting an accounting of all of the funds she had entrusted to his care. Early in their business dealings, he had had Rose Marie sign a power of attorney giving him control over and access to her funds. She did this because of the trust she had in him and because she felt he had the financial ability to secure her future with investments that she simply did not have time to investigate or the desire to assess. Once again she was about to embark on yet another lengthy and expensive legal action. Their mutual friend, LeGrand Richards, predicted beforehand that no one would win, that the "wits" of the attorneys would be the only thing in final question; and he was right. The litigation itself carried on for years.

Rose Marie's life was plagued with painful lawsuits. When she had obtained her annulment from Jack Reid, it was she—not Jack—who suffered financially. Jack drained the Canadian company's assets and held Rose Marie's children "for ransom," demanding payment from her before he would let them go to their mother in California.

In a similar manner, Jack and Nina Kessler recognized Rose Marie's trusting nature early in their relationship. Manipulating the stock in their favor, the Kesslers ultimately reaped a large profit.

They later altered their original oral agreement with Rose Marie, alleging that she had committed to bring $25,000 cash to match their $25,000 initial investment—with the understanding, they said, that she was also expected to contribute her expertise, designs, and patents without compensation or credit for value.

However, Rose Marie had sued and the judge ruled against Kesslers, who were able, nevertheless, to retain most of the company's stock, diluting Rose Marie's original half interest in the company to only ten percent.[1] Winning the case, Rose Marie received a royalty of one percent of the net sales because the suits bore her name. Although the Kesslers didn't realize it at the time, this minor success was to be Rose Marie's salvation. Neither party dreamed that sales would achieve the volume they did.

The Kesslers' next action to limit Rose Marie's royalties was to create the *Western Miss* swimsuit line. They also began manufacturing the *Marina Del Mar* line and selling designs that were Rose Marie Reid originals under a different name. Once again, Rose Marie was forced to file suit again to retain her one percent.

Nina Kessler said to Rose Marie, in the course of one particularly trying lawsuit: "It wasn't 'til we were well into this trial that I found out my husband [Jack] stopped paying tithing and when I knew that, I knew we'd lost."[2]

Said Rose Marie's attorneys: "We don't trust the Kesslers or Haberfeld." And with good reason. According to the suit, the Kesslers and Haberfeld had "unjustly enriched" themselves at Rose Marie's expense.[3] Although Rose Marie "won" the decisions, she was not financially compensated for the losses.

In 1955, Harry A. Cohen, the Rose Marie Reid, Inc., controller, penned an inter-office memo in preparation for yet another lawsuit against Rose Marie. "It is well known to the company management," it stated, "that Mrs. Reid has worked hard to spread the message that all of the success of the company has been attributable to her efforts exclusively."[4]

Cohen then attributed the success of the company to its "coordinated management" team which had arrived after 1949. He acknowledged in particular "Paul Haberfeld as general manager" and of course, "Mr. and Mrs. Kessler," as the factors that really accounted for the company's radical success. He also complimented the "sales and production organization," "skilled administrative talent," the "controller's skill in financial management," and "the employee group."

However true Cohen's memo may have been, without Rose Marie Reid, the company—which had enjoyed an international following in 46 countries and was the world's largest manufacturer of women's swimwear for a decade—folded, at almost exactly the time that Rose Marie walked out the doors.

The case for which the Cohen memo was prepared was "Rose Marie Reid vs. the Commissioner of Internal Revenue," Docket No. 51225. Jack and Nina Kessler and Harry Cohen entered into the case as witnesses against Rose Marie. At issue was whether the sale of patents, designs, and leasing her name, from which her royalties came, could be claimed as capital gains. According to Cohen, it was "the first time" that he had been "made aware that Mrs. Reid had treated any portion of her royalties income as capital gain: a revelation which came as a surprise to [him] indeed."

The sale of Rose Marie's patents, designs, and lease of her name, it was contended, constituted "ordinary income" only. However, Judge Raum determined this claim to be false. Said Raum, "California rules respecting the transfer of a trade name cannot change the nature of the payments into payments for services for the federal income tax purposes, when they were not in fact made for services rendered. Whatever the defects or incapacities of such transfer . . . we are convinced that she received the payments in respect of such transfer, and not for personal services." The U.S. government, Raum declared, had erroneously determined her income as "ordinary income."[5]

Although Rose Marie won the lawsuit, the judgment handed down in compensation was far from adequate, as would always be the case. Nevertheless, the decision was precedent-setting, and for years after, many cases used the landmark decision to strengthen their own arguments in tax cases.

Tragically, the most extensive lawsuit Rose Marie was forced to endure was the one she felt compelled to bring against her friend and accountant, Michael Silver. No one had suspected any wrongdoing until the early 1960s. Even then, the only reason Rose Marie had asked Silver for an accounting was because she and her son, Bruce, had become involved in several financial ventures, and they found it necessary to reconcile her financial matters. For this reason, Bruce encouraged Rose Marie to ask for an accounting from Michael Silver.

Rose Marie asked Bruce's attorney, Kline Strong, to press Silver for an accounting. By July it was evident that Silver had taken large amounts from Rose Marie; amounts as large as $140,445 had been transferred to Silver's personal accounts which should have gone to Rose Marie's accounts. From 1953 to 1962, Silver received cash in excess of $1,450,000 (equal to $6,554,000 in 1991 dollars) directly from Rose Marie's share of the Rose Marie Reid company's earnings. He used the money to purchase property in his own name, to build his home, and to buy stock for his wife.

Strong wrote pointed and exacting letters to Silver: "If this is an investment, on what date or dates did the borrowing occur and how much was each borrowing? Did the borrowing bear interest? When was it repaid?"[6] There was no response from Silver.

Rose Marie obtained the services of Stafford Grady, the Los Angeles attorney who had represented her so well in previous cases, and they began an inquiry. Both Strong and Grady recommended that Rose Marie obtain legal counsel in Chicago because Silver was licensed in Chicago. Rose Marie directed them to hire her an attorney with the sole stipulation that they were not to hire a Mormon. Her reason was more charitable than Silver deserved: "If Michael ever does go to church again, I see no reason for casting a shadow on him in anyone's mind."[7]

Gerald Snyder, the Chicago attorney, soon found serious deficiencies in Silver's handling of Rose Marie's affairs. "The more we delve into Silver," said Snyder, "the more we realize that your client has been in hands which are highly suspect."[8]

They learned that Silver had had several other illegal deals going while handling Rose Marie's funds. An associate, Newton Feldman, had helped Silver carry off a Florida transaction by issuing a "phony second mortgage," in which Feldman had made $45,000. "Michael Silver is following a pattern in getting your client [Rose Marie] to sign a power of attorney," said Snyder. "[Silver] did this with

Newton Feldman. A great deal of difficulty arose; Silver demanded and received $10,000 to get out of the matter. Newton Feldman died and his sister said in open court, 'Michael Silver, you're a crook and you'll live to regret it!'"[9]

They learned that Silver was also being investigated for writing checks on other people's accounts besides Rose Marie's. "As hard-hitting as are the allegations in the complaint filed in federal court against Michael Silver, it now appears that those allegations may be understatements," wrote Snyder to Rose Marie's attorney.

As events began to unravel, Silver became sick and was unavailable for much of the difficult questioning. Silver's attorney, Jess Raban, tried to answer for his client. He even produced properties on paper from the companies he alleged could be refinanced "to obtain a substantial amount of cash for Mrs. Reid."[10] Raban came up with only vague estimates of real value, however, and as late as 16 August 1962, Silver was still signing Rose Marie's name to transact business. Strong and Grady demanded adamantly that this be stopped, fearing that Silver was "manufacturing" expenses in several accounts.[11] Large amounts of cash transfers were unexplainable, and reconstructing a cash flow was difficult, if not impossible.

By 24 August 1962, Strong had successfully executed a letter terminating the services of Michael Silver. Next, Strong went after the assets Silver had conveniently amassed for his alleged borrowings against his joint accounts with Rose Marie. Strong communicated to Snyder that "the 'borrowing' arrangement which Silver imposed upon Rose Marie Reid can be unmasked and defeated." In the terminating letter to Silver, Strong demanded a "complete and accurate accounting" of all financial matters Silver had undertaken for Rose Marie during a period of nearly ten years.[12] "It will be expected that you shall have an accounting by Tuesday, September 4, 1962,"[13] Strong said, intending Silver to believe he meant seriously to sue. However, the tersely worded statement had an opposite effect.

Silver stormed back at Strong through Raban. Silver had a legally binding contract with Rose Marie until 1966, he said, and he refused to accept the termination of his power of attorney. He also refused to meet with Strong to discuss any of the affairs. He was in the process of "compiling information," he claimed, and would submit such only to Stafford Grady when it was ready.[14]

To this, Strong replied: "You are advised that any action . . . taken after . . . August 24, 1962, will be deemed a wholly voluntary act [for which you] shall be held responsible. . . . Govern yourself accordingly."[15] At this, Silver transferred large amounts of cash from the American National Bank of Chicago into his own accounts. Rose Marie had no other choice; she was forced to take court action.

On 2 November 1962, a complaint was filed on behalf of Rose Marie against Michael Silver in the federal district court. Knowing well the impact this would have, Rose Marie considered this decision no small matter.

Her old friend LeGrand Richards wrote: "I dislike to contemplate what the result of this suit could be. You cannot take your money with you when you go. . . . I would like to believe that you are both honest, and if someone could sit down and go over matters with you, I think you could come to an adjustment. . . . I love you both. You have been such wonderful friends. . . . I have always had a feeling that in the courts it is not so much a question of right and wrong as it is the wits of the attorneys."[16]

Elder Richards, however, did not understand the extent of Silver's duplicity and the length of time Rose Marie's lawyers had taken attempting to get Silver to render a proper accounting. Certainly Rose Marie would rather have done anything than bring suit against this man who had been her close friend for so long. He was very nearly a brother to her, and she felt like she was suing a family member. She had no choice, however; his power of attorney had to be revoked.

She asked Strong to explain the situation to Elder Richards. Strong called him immediately to set up an appointment to discuss "the Silver suit." His intent was "to bring to Elder Richards a full realization of the flagrant dishonesty of Michael Silver in handling [Rose Marie's] affairs and the fact that we negotiated for several months with him . . . to avoid a lawsuit or any publicity."[17]

But the lawsuit did attract publicity, and *The Chicago American* even attempted to create a love triangle out of the case.[18]

In court, Silver admitted that a fiduciary relationship had existed between himself and Rose Marie—he had received "maybe"

$1,432,345.83 in cash directly from the Rose Marie Reid company, and Rose Marie may have given him another half million from other personal funds, "but he couldn't tell how much more."[19] He also admitted that he had kept no journal of disbursements other than his checkbook, no journal of receipts other than check stubs, no ledger accounts showing receipt of monies, and no general ledger account for the entire period.[20]

Silver alleged that he had turned over to Rose Marie about $328,000 in miscellaneous investments of real estate, joint ventures, bank balances, and an outstanding loan due Rose Marie. He alleged that Rose Marie did not acknowledge even these returns; Rose Marie denied that she had ever received any evidence of these investments. She continued to press for an accounting of all funds, but Silver would not account. He claimed that he had record of over 1,000 phone calls to her and had visited her Los Angeles home on numerous occasions, and had therefore rendered an accounting. For these alleged services Silver had charged Rose Marie $90,000 ($406,800 in 1991 dollars) for his advice as her "business manager" and another $72,000 ($325,440 in 1991 dollars) for "accounting services." Clearly he had built for himself an estate in his own name of at least $200,000 (which at that time was the equivalent of some two million dollars).[21] The rest of the money could not be accounted for.

On July 30, 1963, Judge Igoe turned the whole affair over to a Special Master, Ralph J. Gutgsell. After several months, Gutgsell "recommended the entry of a decree requiring the Defendant [Silver] to file an accounting in writing, setting out all receipts of money, property, or undivided interests therein ever owned by the Plaintiff [Rose Marie] or in which the Plaintiff had any interest coming into the possession or control of the Defendant; that the Defendant state all of his acts and doings with respect to Plaintiff's property, including all receipts, disbursements, and distributions therefrom, that the Defendant file appropriate receipts and vouchers evidencing all disbursements and distributions." He then asked for $25,000 for his services.[22]

Silver strongly objected to the report and undertook to show that he had rendered an accounting through his many phone calls and visits. Judge Igoe ordered Gutgsell to look again at the evidence.

After more testimony, which amounted to well over 2,000 pages, Gutgsell filed a second report stating that "no particular system of keeping trust records" is required; "where the agent has rendered periodical accounts" that is sufficient; and that the court should require "no further accounting."[23]

Rose Marie and her attorneys were horrified. Believing that the conclusion was erroneous and suspecting some manner of duplicity, they immediately filed an appeal. The appeal cited thirty-five precedent cases to the effect that (1) "a trustee is under a duty to keep clear, distinct, and accurate accounts, and to render a complete accounting to the beneficiary"; and (2) "All obscurities and doubts are to be taken adversely to a trustee who fails to keep clear, distinct, and accurate accounts."

Snyder also demanded that Silver pay all court costs and fees due the Special Master and alleged that Silver's defense testimony constituted an "unjustified attack upon the Plaintiff." He asked that the original finding of the Master be upheld, that the lost funds be restored, and that damages to Rose Marie's character be compensated.

The appeal was tried on 28 December 1965, before Judge Hastings, who concluded that Gutgsell's report was in error: Silver had not rendered an accounting by law, and the Master's fees were excessive. But the fees were allowed to stand; each party was to pay half. Hastings then remanded the case to the district court to force Silver to render a full accounting.

Rose Marie found it all too much—another trial to decide what so easily could have been decided earlier. Elder Richards had foreseen the unhappy result of the trial long before it had occurred. The case died somewhere in the labyrinth of the halls of "justice."

Although Rose Marie "won," it was a hollow victory. She paid over $150,000 in legal fees (over $1 million in 1992 dollars). There was nothing to recover. All funds had been transferred, and ultimately she received $5,000 in compensation from Silver. She also received the hard-earned termination of Silver's contract as one holding her power of attorney. Only the courts and the attorneys received any benefits. No one to date has ever recovered the lost $1.5 million. Snyder later wrote from Chicago that he was sending Rose Marie a check for $429.39 which he recovered from one of her accounts, and another check for $136.81 from a second.[24]

Despite the $150,000 in court fees and the discovery that the money she hoped to recover was already lost, Marion said of Rose Marie: "You still never heard Rose Marie speak evil of Michael Silver. She simply said, 'The Lord will take care of him, I don't have to.'"

Marion continued, "[Rose Marie] was too busy to take care of her own business affairs. Her own requests were small, and the money was too available. If it hadn't been Michael Silver, it would have been another like him. . . . She always trusted too much. She permitted the temptation to be too great."

This was the reason Judge Hastings made Rose Marie pay half of the Master's fee. Knowing of her shrewd business sense, he simply could not understand why she had let Silver and others dupe her.

Nevertheless, Rose Marie never knew anything but trust, even from this costly and damaging experience. She gave too much and blamed herself if somehow her giving turned out negatively. She repeated the same mistake over and over again. The effects of this costly court experience did not change her basic nature; she simply believed in the honesty of all people and she always gave too much license and freedom to those representing her. She never wanted to return to court, however. Years later, when she was forced into settlement proceedings in the case of "R and M Living Wigs," she would come to a settlement only by arbitration.

During the final years of her life, Rose Marie was assisted greatly by Dean Chipman, her friend and financial counselor. A blessing of integrity for fifteen years, Dean was her accountant and representative until her death. Always impressed by her "generosity and her boundless trust," Dean refused numerous offers from her to have power of attorney over her affairs, saying "that was not a sound business relationship." When she tried to persuade him "to use [his] own discretion with her funds," he said, "I replied that I feel I am an honest man, and no man should have that privilege over another person's finances."[25]

The Silver tragedy, combined with the losses suffered from Bruce's failed business ventures and the money she gave to others, left Rose Marie Reid almost completely impoverished. It would seem nearly impossible to imagine that blessings could have resulted from the Silver lawsuit, but Rose Marie concluded: "The Lord . . . probably want[ed] my children to have the thrill of rescuing me, and of personal achievement which they will have starting from nothing, and which they could not have if they had to compete with a successful mother."[26]

Notes

1. IRS tax brief, 21 June 1956, Docket No. 51225
2. Sharon Alden, as quoted in Rose Marie Reid's Oral History, p. 31.
3. Lyon & Lyon to Rose Marie Reid, 24 April 1961.
4. Harry A. Cohen, memorandum, 15 September 1955.
5. Tax brief, Docket No. 51225.
6. Kline Strong, certified letter to Michael Silver, 24 August 1962.
7. Rose Marie Reid, letter to Kline Strong and Stafford Grady, 14 July 1962.
8. Gerald Snyder, letter to Kline Strong, 13 November 1962
9. Ibid.
10. Jess Raban, letter to Stafford Grady, 18 July 1962.
11. Kline Strong, letter to Stafford Grady, 16 August 1962.
12. Strong to Silver, 24 August 1962.
13. Ibid.
14. Jess Raban, letter to Kline Strong, 28 August 1962.
15. Kline Strong, letter to Jess Raban, 14 September 1962.
16. LeGrand Richards, letter to Rose Marie Reid, 5 December 1962.
17. Kline Strong, letter to Rose Marie Reid, 18 December 1962.
18. Kline Strong, letter to Rose Marie Reid, 6 November 1962.
19. Appellate Case No. 14884, p. 25.
20. Ibid., p. 23
21. Ibid., p. 24
22. Ibid., p. 7.
23. Ibid., p. 22.
24. Ibid.
25. Dean Chipman, interview, 20 February 1992. All subsequent comments by Dean Chipman are taken from this source.
26. Rose Marie Reid, letter to Kline Strong, 14 July 1962.

Rose Marie modeling an R & M living wig.

CHAPTER 18

R & M Living Wigs

Rose Marie anticipated a quiet retirement in Provo, Utah, where she had brought her mother before her death in 1965. However, Rose Marie continued to encounter financial difficulties in the building of her home. The foundation alone cost $50,000, at a time when entire homes didn't sell for as much. The architect then approached the family with the news that the actual costs would exceed the projected cost by $100,000. How would Rose Marie and her family deal with this costly error? The half-finished home, said Carole's husband, Jim Burr, was "draining her financially."

Rose Marie's health was also steadily declining, dating from her hospitalization for the bleeding ulcer. The sponge left in her body during that initial operation caused extensive damage to her lungs, and the resultant asthma was so severe that she required constant medication the rest of her life. Following her long hospital stay, Rose Marie's health slowly improved; but it took a full year for her to regain her strength from the near-fatal surgery.

During one visit to New York, while working with the Jonathan Logan Company to whom she had licensed her name and her designs, Rose Marie was caught in the famous New York City blackout. It occurred at the peak of the afternoon rush hour when Rose Marie was thirty blocks from her hotel and could not get a taxi. After walking to the hotel, Rose Marie was given a candle by the desk clerk so she could find her way to her room on the fortieth floor.

After she had ascended only a few floors, however, the candle blew out, and she was forced to finish her climb in complete darkness. Her asthma made her fight for every breath, and she thought she'd go insane with exhaustion and fear. With each step she'd pray, asking the Lord to get her to her room. Somehow she at last made it to the correct floor and to her room, but the terror and fatigue she felt did not pass.

Her asthma was so severe that she spent a great deal of time in the hospital as the years passed. The prescribed medication caused severe side effects, and the doctors discovered that Rose Marie could only tolerate about eight different foods. Furthermore, because she had become allergic to nearly all chemicals, the food that she could eat needed to be organically grown.

Rose Marie had a young friend, Janet Compton, who lived near her in Provo and would prove to be her salvation. Interestingly, Janet's mother, June, had heard Rose Marie speak at the height of her career. In comparison to this poised, confident woman, the young June had felt highly inadequate. After the speech, June's friend wanted her to go with her up to meet Rose Marie. June declined, thinking, "Rose Marie Reid wouldn't bother with someone as ordinary and insignificant as I am." Nevertheless, June had been surprised that Rose Marie wanted to live in Provo, Utah, someday, as she had mentioned in her speech.[1]

Years later, when Rose Marie did at last move to Provo, by coincidence she moved into June's very neighborhood and attended the same ward (church congregation) that June did. Rose Marie was asked to be a teacher in the Young Women's organization, to which June's daughter Janet belonged.

As Rose Marie worked with Janet, she learned that this young woman was having a difficult time understanding and accepting that Joseph Smith had received a visit from God the Father and his son Jesus Christ, as taught by the Mormon Church. In fact, Janet found herself even questioning the very existence of God. Knowing this, Rose Marie took a special interest in Janet. When Janet expressed her doubts, Rose Marie shook her finger at her and said very firmly, "You know better than that!" As Janet grew to know her and feel her love, she began to realize the truth of the things she had been taught.

Janet knew that Rose Marie wasn't well. "She is dying," Janet said to her mother. "You should see her! She is starving to death." Although organically grown food was not widely available at that time, Janet decided to search the area for food that Rose Marie could tolerate. June tried to dissuade Janet, remembering how intimidated she had felt by this great woman. Surely Rose Marie wouldn't want to be bothered by them, June told her daughter. Rose Marie's daughter Carole was taking good care of her mother.

But Janet was not to be dissuaded. "This is something I have to do," she said to her mother. "I feel a compulsion that I can't explain." Janet and her father scoured the area in search of organically grown food, not returning home until 2:00 a.m. with the back seat of the car loaded with the foods they had sought. Rose Marie's daughter Carole was very thankful as, indeed, she could *not* have taken care of it for her mother. The mother of five young children, Carole was pregnant with her sixth, and the burden of constantly caring for Rose Marie had nearly undone her.

Janet and her mother, June, helped care for Rose Marie that entire summer. When Rose Marie felt like giving up, Janet, in a familiar echo, would shake her finger at her and say, "You know better than that!" Together, they loved Rose Marie back to health.

Although her physical and emotional energies were torn in so many directions, Rose Marie continued to combine her instinct for business, her flair for creating beauty, and her concern for a woman's appearance in swim attire. She was especially sympathetic to the never-ending concern women felt about what swimming did to their hairstyles. Even Rose Marie's daughters gave up swimming in the family pool—"it was always a concern whether there was enough time to reset, dry, and style our hair," they said. The Rose Marie Reid Company had designed fashionable accessories that included bathing caps, but they never shared the success of Rose Marie's swimsuits. The caps did not keep hair dry enough to maintain the style, and for many people they were simply too uncomfortable to wear. The options were simply a scarf, a bathing hat, or wet, unstyled hair.

Rose Marie always felt that a natural-looking wig was the logical resolution to the problem. As the Rose Marie Reid Company grew more precarious, Rose Marie and her son, Bruce, began to seriously consider the idea of marketing wigs. The more they discussed the potential for the wig market, the more feasible the idea seemed. Together they decided that he should go to New York and investigate purchasing an already-existing company. So Bruce, along with a young and promising business student from Brigham Young University named Gary Meredith, traveled to New York and approached a few well-known companies. Gary would later recall the ease with which Bruce met and talked with accomplished business executives. There were never any reservations about going to the companies' owners and presidents.

In fact, one of the first things necessary was to establish a financial institution in New York where they would do their banking, so they went straight to the Chase Manhattan Bank. They asked for an interview with the president, and in a few minutes they were sitting across the desk from David Rockefeller. Said Gary, "Bruce didn't have the slightest hesitation or feeling of inferiority."[2]

After investigating a few wig companies, Bruce and Gary concluded that the existing wigs were problematic. Real hair wigs were heavy, lacked luster, and were usually imported from Europe. The alternative synthetic wigs looked like an accessory to a Halloween costume. So Bruce and Gary decided that instead of buying an existing wig company, they would investigate the possibility of manufacturing a new and innovative wig that would share none of those problems.

They met with Professor Milton Frishman at the Union Carbide Company and told him what they were looking for. In time, Frishman developed a beautiful synthetic fiber that could be made into hair pieces that took minimal care—one that men and women could put on like a mesh cap. The wig weighed only two ounces, and the hair was looped through each stitch of the cap instead of being sewn in rows.

The new wigs were a great success. Women loved the freedom that a wig gave them, and men found the toupee to be natural and easy to wear.

The new company was named "The R & M Living Wig"—the

"R" for Reid, the "M" for Meredith. The wigs recreated natural-looking hair that was easy to handle. The "new miracle hair," a synthetic fiber called D-40 modacrylic, replaced the costly and almost unobtainable human hair wigs imported from Europe. The fiber came in 20 different colors, was very lightweight, and would not absorb odors or fade in color.

At the time of purchase, the wig was styled and matched to the buyer's own hair style. Women were instructed to take the wigs home and see if their husbands could tell the difference. Husbands appreciated how quickly their wives were ready to go and how free they were to do activities that had previously restricted them because of their hair.

The husbands, however, had predictable reactions to wigs. "If a woman's husband comes to the store," said Rose Marie, "he usually wants her to be a blonde." Or if he didn't see it styled and placed on her head, he would usually say, "Take it off!"

The wigs were initially promoted as a fun way to change hairstyles, but soon Rose Marie realized she was marketing a very useful product. "At first I thought of the fun women would have with it," she said, "but I found there were a greater number of women with thinning hair who needed and wanted a wig."[3] Besides full wigs, R & M carried a full line of wiglets, half wigs, and toupees.

Clare Middlemiss, the secretary to President David O. McKay (of the Mormon church), wrote to tell Rose Marie how her wigs eased her stressful and busy life: "Usually at general conference time [the semi-annual conference for the entire Mormon Church], I am beside myself wondering how I am going to find time to get to a beauty shop to get my hair properly taken care of, but this conference I had not a worry in the world in this respect, because I knew in that little carrying case was my 'hair-do' all ready for me. I just cannot tell you what it has meant to me to have this freedom."[4]

Rose Marie stressed how easy it was to care for these wigs. "The care of the wig was effortless, just a little detergent [and] squish the wig in water as you would nylon stockings. Then just add a little vinegar in the last rinse." It should be drip-dried, she advised, "hanging from the bathtub tap." When it was dry, it bounced back with curl ready to be styled again. It never needed rollers. "It only takes friends 15 minutes to get used to you in a wig, 30 minutes for its wearer, and an hour for husbands," said Rose Marie. One husband commented that it was the best present his wife ever gave him. "When I wanted to go out, she said her hair wasn't done and she couldn't go. Now she is always ready to go out."[5]

Rose Marie said to Helen King that the Lord had given her the wigs just in time. "[The closing of Rose Marie Reid International] did not happen until wigs were really going well. . . . [They] look so great we have had to double our estimates for the next three months. The figures they are planning look fantastic."[6]

The real debut for the company in May 1963, when R & M Living Wigs opened with a big promotion in Saks Fifth Avenue in New York. "It was a very pressured time for everyone," said Carole, who came out with Rose Marie from Provo. "We worked hard preparing the wigs at night so we could style them on the customers the next day. Mother worked right beside the operators during the day, and then we stayed up all night to get ready for the next day."

The wig company, however, was only one of Bruce's interests. This was very frustrating to his lawyer, Kline Strong. In a letter to Rose Marie, Strong wrote, "Bruce has too many ideas and yet he doesn't do the work himself."[7]

To this Rose Marie replied, always in defense of Bruce, "I . . . listened to the 'he doesn't work' until I had to say, 'I read that there are two kinds of people—those who do all the work themselves and so are limited in what they can accomplish, and those who have brains enough to surround themselves with other people who can do many times the work. Bruce has done the latter. He has an excellent sales organization all working on the wigs. . . . Gary [Meredith] and Frank Saunders are producing the best wigs in the world. Bruce has the ability to choose the right people, and he has made few mistakes.'"[8]

Rose Marie was always concerned that Bruce would not get the credit he deserved. "I am sure," she said, "that Mother and Aunt Florence have said to Bruce that without me the wigs wouldn't be where they are. And that's not true. He had the organization before I went east. I maybe got them into Saks a little faster than they would have. But a few weeks more and they'd have done it. So I don't deserve the credit. Bruce wants a success that is apart from me."[9]

Working closely with his mother during the opening at Saks Fifth Avenue was hard for Bruce. It was difficult for the store to rely on Rose Marie Reid's son; they preferred to work directly with the internationally famous designer. Bruce finally asked Rose Marie to leave. "We left exhausted," remembered Carole, "and flew home hoping to let Bruce continue running the company on his own. Mother had always told us how hard it is to be in business with family members, and I certainly saw exactly what she meant while in New York."

Soon, however, Bruce decided to pursue his other interests. In order to do this, he decided to sell his investment in the wig company to two existing stockholders, New York advertisers Jack Armstrong and Jim Wickersham, who then owned 20 percent of the company. Rose Marie was to receive a continuing royalty interest in the wig company if Bruce sold his shares to Armstrong and Wickersham, although they would then hold the controlling interest. This left Rose Marie in the same predicament she had endured with the Kesslers.

Gary Meredith suggested that he purchase the controlling interest for $75,000; this way Rose Marie's interests would be protected. At the formation of the company, Brigham Young University had been given twenty-two percent of the company, with President Earnest L. Wilkinson sitting as chairman of the board of directors. All of these details were handled by Kline Strong, acting as a fiduciary for the company. Bruce, satisfied with the arrangement, left to pursue a business in Alaska, and Rose Marie went to Provo to see about relocating her mother and Aunt Florence.

Nine months later, in October 1964, Bruce returned and discovered that the instructions he thought he had left for the wig company had been entirely controverted. Instead of Gary Meredith having control of the lucrative company, Kline Strong, his attorney and fiduciary, was now in control. His mother had been reduced to a nonvoting patent holder, with only a royalty interest in the company. Several independent corporations, owned by the original company, had been created and named *Suzanne*, after Strong's wife.

Bruce was shocked to find the same legal problems continually plaguing his family. Once again, a fiduciary, supposedly representing the family interests, had enhanced his own position at their expense. But Rose Marie simply didn't have the heart or mind for another lawsuit. They instead agreed to a settlement by arbitration.

Since Brigham Young University's twenty-two percent amounted to 6,600 shares of the R & M stock, all parties involved agreed to have President Ernest L. Wilkinson and Albert Bowen, both affiliated with the university and lawyers themselves, hear the case. All agreed to abide by their decision.

The arbitration took place in January of 1965. A Mr. Ashton represented Strong, with Arthur Nielsen representing the Reids. Following nearly twenty hours of testimony, the arbitrators found that Strong had used his fiduciary relationship in a questionable manner, but not illegally.

The decision of the arbitrators was concluded more to Brigham Young University's advantage than either Rose Marie's or Strong's. This was done by removing the royalty payments for the owners. In so doing, it created more working capital and made the company a very attractive business to purchase. Shortly thereafter, thirty very successful venture capitalists from the First National Bank of Boston purchased the company for $7 million.

Armstrong and Wickersheim received $600,000. Strong received $600,000. Bruce and Rose Marie received $3.5 million plus the ownership of the men's division, Crown Toupee. Another $1.2 million was put into the company for working capital. Gary Meredith retained his stock and his position as president of the company. BYU was given the option of selling its stock for $1.2 million dollars or retaining the stock.

President Wilkinson opted to keep their stock as an investment for the university, allowing himself to remain as the chairman of the board. Wilkinson obviously thought the value would increase, but more importantly, he desired to have the university associated with the venture capitalists, thus creating the opportunity to benefit BYU with other financial opportunities and investments.

The wig company continued to do very well. By 1966 the sales were in excess of $10 million, and the company had one thousand employees.[10]

To replace the royalties taken from her, Rose Marie was given the men's division of R & M Living Wigs, Crown Toupee. She recognized it as an opportunity for her daughter Sharon and her husband, Paul. She moved back to California and started working immediately with Sharon and Paul to set up a marketing organization. Night after night, Paul and Rose Marie would travel to make special contacts, then stay up until late making hair-swatch sample books. Once again, Rose Marie seemed tireless. David, her eight-year-old grandson, even volunteered to get up at 1:00 a.m. and help her with the process. She wasn't tireless, however; in fact, she soon became very tired and ill, and it was necessary for Carole to come to Los Angeles and take her home to Utah where she could get medical treatment from her own doctors. Paul continued to manage the toupee company, and sold it a few years later.

"If Mother could have lived forever, the ideas for successful businesses would have never ceased," said Carole confidently. "Her mind worked constantly; it was only her body that slowed down. She had a creative brilliance coupled with an inner drive to produce results, and if you didn't keep up with her, soon you were left in the wake of accomplishment."

Notes

1. June Compton, interview, n.d.
2. Gary Meredith, interview, 8 February 1992. All subsequent comments by Gary Meredith are taken from this source.
3. Charlotte Leigh Taylor, *West L.A. Independent Press*, 29 July 1965, n.p.
4. Clare Middlemiss, letter to Rose Marie Reid, 11 June 1966.
5. Taylor, *West L.A. Independent Press*, n.p.
6. Rose Marie Reid, letter to Helen King, n.d.
7. Kline Strong, letter to Rose Marie Reid, n.d.
8. Rose Marie Reid, letter to Helen King, n.d.
9. Ibid.
10. *California Apparel News*, 6 May 1966; see also Gary Meredith, interview.

CHAPTER 19

A Sacred Honor

Rose Marie was always conscious of the needs of others. One day she met a woman who told her that she and her husband had lost everything they owned in a bank foreclosure and had come to live in Orem, Utah, from Nampa, Idaho, on a shoestring. They had left behind a shed full of empty fruit bottles, which they sorely needed for canning fruit for their family. Hearing the story, Rose Marie immediately wrote to Marion in Baker, Oregon.

"They had to leave their many fruit bottles stored in someone's barn there," she said. "They need them. . . . If you are driving, without a car full, could you stop and pick them up? Even if you have to get a small U-Haul trailer. There are a great lot of them. She will pay for the trailer by working for you."[1]

Although it would have been easier and more economical to buy new bottles, Rose Marie hated the thought of wasting the empty bottles in someone's barn. She knew, too, that it would be better for the woman not to be the recipient of charity. That alone was worth the work to do the deed, and Marion could then have the joy of doing some service, carefully planned by Rose Marie.

Once a young woman appeared at Rose Marie's door. The stranger asked if she could speak to Rose Marie a moment, and Rose Marie invited her in. The young woman and her husband were struggling students; she had only one more semester until she would graduate and could support him. She had nowhere to turn. "Would you lend me just enough for tuition for one semester?" she begged. Rose Marie wrote her a check on the spot.

Years later this woman related to Rose Marie's daughter Carole that she had never gotten over her mother's kindness to someone she had never seen before. Carole heard many such stories after her mother's death.

Carole also learned how her mother had lent one woman the money for a down payment on a house. The woman was Jewish and had been disinherited from her family when she married a Catholic. The woman told Rose Marie that she could only afford to make $30 payments on this loan. "Mother always told me how much she appreciated the doctor who allowed her to make $10 payments for delivering her babies," Carole said. "She made them for years."

Every month, on the same day, the $30 payment would arrive in the mail. "Mother always said, 'She was one of the few people who ever paid her back—and she wasn't even Mormon!'"

Rose Marie was one of the first celebrities to move to Provo, and people were fascinated by her. Her property joined Carole's, and their houses were side by side. "We always said that if we had a quarter for every car that turned around in our cul de sac, we could pay off both of our houses," laughed Carole.

Because of this interest, the ward Relief Society approached Rose Marie with the idea of a home tour, using her house and Carole's, to raise money for the building of the new Provo temple. Rose Marie and Carole, along with her entire family, temporarily vacated their homes for two days while visitors streamed through their houses. The Relief Society charged a dollar admission and rasied nearly $2000 for the temple fund.

Strangers frequently came to Rose Marie's door just to meet her. Some even requested a tour through her home, which she gave them. Often people whom no one in the family knew could be found sitting in her living room, where Rose Marie would talk to them about their families and their lives.

"One day we were sitting in her family room watching television during the momentous event when the first space craft landed on the moon," said Carole. "We were captivated, waiting for Neil

Armstrong's first steps. Her doorbell rang, and two people said they were in the neighborhood and would like to have a tour through her home."

Rose Marie surprised them with her response. "You can't mean that you would want to see my house when at this very moment one of the great historical events of all time is happening. Please come in and watch the first steps ever taken on the moon."

Said Carole, "The two people chose not to come in and left, and Mother was shocked to learn that her home had more appeal to someone than the moon."

In 1971, Rose Marie tried to sell her home in Provo. She realized that it had been a mistake to build it on such a grand scale, and that it would be hard to sell it for what it was worth. Elder Richards, not in an unkind manner, but out of love, wrote: "I don't know whether there is anyone in the state of Utah who has enough money that they could purchase your beautiful home, for it is beautiful. When you built it, you had no idea that you would want to sell it or I am sure you would not have spent the sum that you did."[2]

Rose Marie lamented the fortune she lost to Michael Silver, the $80,000 in goods lost to Jack Reid, and now the loss of her house. She worried that the Jonathan Logan contract would end, as it provided her a livelihood in her retirement years. At one time Logan did send a representative to her, with the result that the contract was altered and her income reduced by fifty percent. That was the last negotiating she ever wanted to participate in. She no longer had the will to negotiate contracts with her usual intensity, and she refused to even consider another lawsuit. After that, she always sent her daughters, Sharon or Carole, to negotiate for her.

To Marion she confided, "My insurance policies all have such big loans on them . . . all I pay is interest. This month I need $20,000 . . . and all I own is $1490. . . . Imagine $1490 is my whole fortune!"[3]

"To lose another fortune on this place would be normal. Please use your prayers a thousand times a day for me," she said. Eventually she was able to sell her home to a family from Florida for about half its worth. Later, the musical Osmond family would buy it.

Rose Marie filled her time with speaking engagements, genealogy, and her grandchildren. She communicated frequently with her friends. She enjoyed her visits with Cleon Skousen, historian and scholar, who frequently visited, bringing with him his wife, Jewel. Skousen shared Rose Marie's interest in the Jewish people and had written numerous books relative to Israel, Zionism, and the future of the Jewish people in connection with Mormonism. While a professor of religion at Brigham Young University, Skousen had traveled to Israel twenty-five times.

Rose Marie's respect for men such as Cleon Skousen may have been heightened by her own failed marriages. It was a comfort for her to know that men of quality really did exist, in addition to her father—men who were kind and gentle, who contemplated godly things and realized that the highest rewards of life were intellectual and spiritual, rather than material.

Truman G. Madsen, at the time a very young mission president in New England, wrote to say, "How often we talk of you and how nostalgic are our recollections of the Church history tour and the wonderful days spent under your wing at South Bundy. You've really brushed a wave of warmth and comfort into my life which I can never forget."[4]

His letter also contains a detailed response in answer to something Rose Marie had written about the Prophet Joseph Smith. They spoke of the Prophet's children, and whether or not he had any living descendants in the Church. Such a lovely, warm letter from a budding, young scholar to an older, but still vibrant, beautiful, famous Mormon woman must have refreshed Rose Marie.

Her correspondents also included President Wilkinson of Brigham Young University. Rose Marie was more deeply involved in making Brigham Young University what it is today than most people realize. Together, she and President Wilkinson participated in many financial arrangements that established the large financial base from which the university operates today.

Rose Marie also communicated with Elder John A. Widtsoe. At one time, Elder Widtsoe wrote in response to a question Rose Marie posed about sleeping in church (referring, no doubt, to a time when she was working night and day and the sleep referred to was the only sleep she found). Elder Widstoe's letter is a classic. "Dear Sister," he wrote, "the problem that you present I am unable to solve for you. Many people have the same disposition, and very often they defend themselves by the simple statement that the best place to sleep is in Church and its meetings. Aside from my jocular remark, however, many people use materials that cause wakefulness. I think if I were you, I would talk the matter over again with your doctor and secure from him a prescription to help you. When a speaker deals with something interesting to you, you will find it easier to keep awake, of course, but that you cannot always control."[5]

One of Rose Marie's most cherished experiences occurred when the president and prophet of the Mormon Church, David O. McKay asked her, through Belle Spafford, then general president of the Relief Society, to redesign the temple garments so people, women especially, would feel more comfortable wearing them. Temple garments are worn by members of the Mormon Church as a symbol of the covenants they make with God to be obedient to his commandments and to strive to live worthy of His protection and guidance. President McKay wanted the women of the Church to love wearing their temple garments, and knowing of Rose Marie's gift in making beautiful swimwear, he asked if she could share her talents with the Church. Rose Marie considered the experience a sacred honor.

At the time of this request, Rose Marie was still living in her home on Bundy Drive in Brentwood, and for this demanding and very extensive project, she set up two large tables in the large family room. The tables remained in place for two years. Night after night Jan would cut, and Rose Marie would design. Patterns hung all over the room, for every size, men's and women's.

Rose Marie did everything possible to make the patterns perfect in fit and fabric. Her task—the most sacred one she could imagine—was one directly for her God. Interestingly, during the process Rose Marie discovered that she was related to Elizabeth Warner Allred, who had made the very first garments of this dispensation in Nauvoo, at the request of Joseph Smith. She wondered if the Lord "[kept] that privilege in one family."[6] Whether or not this was true, she most definitely considered her work on the temple garment to be a divine assignment.

Rose Marie was determined that people would love wearing garments like beautiful lingerie. She researched extensively the Church members' likes and dislikes with regard to the fit of the garments, and invited many friends to her home for dinner just to get their opinions. Rose Marie added lace, and also made maternity and nursing garments. Her good friend, Robert Derx, of Vanity Fair, one of the finest lingerie companies in the world, arranged for lovely, long-lasting fabrics.

For two years Jan Warner and Rose Marie worked on this project. When they had finished teaching missionary lessons, usually around ten or eleven in the evening, they would go into the family room and work on the garment patterns until two or three in the morning.

The end result was the first accurately sized temple garments using standard patterns in the history of the Mormon Church. The Church also began manufacturing the temple garments on its own, a difficult process to manage because of the many people involved in the manufacturing. Working on such a large scale, it was a challenge to stay true to the patterns and proper sizing.

It soon became clear that one of the most requested styles was a two-piece garment for women. Rose Marie made the appeal for this through Sister Spafford to President McKay, but was refused. Knowing of the great demand for a two-piece garment, Rose was disappointed that she couldn't design a two-piece garment to meet the needs of women. "When I die," she said firmly, "I will ask the Lord to approve it." Within a year after her death, when two-piece garments were finally approved, the family just smiled. "That was mother," said Sharon, "always having the courage to go straight to the top."

Even as she grew older and her health grew worse, Rose Marie's energy was difficult to keep up with or even tolerate. Her family often called her mode of operation "organized chaos." Rose Marie could see numerous tasks to be accomplished at one time, and she would attack them all. To be with her at times was exhausting. Always, she was conscious of the value of money, even during the years that her company was most successful.

During one brief vacation while she visited with Marion and Sanford in Baker, Oregon, Rose Marie showed her continual thrift. Apparently Marion invited her sister to take some apples home, saying "They'll spoil if you don't." So Rose Marie, leaving early the next morning and not wanting to wake Marion, wrote the following note on the back of a scrap of paper:

"My darling sister and brother. You are the dearest people who ever lived and thank you for everything. (1) I sorted out the rotten apples and am taking the wilted ones. (2) Next year do not just put them in a box with plastic over. Put them inside two of those dress weight plastics and tie tightly. Then in the box in the garage, they are like fresh picked. I will peel all the way to Boise & Velva [Elvie Jr.'s wife] can cook and have those; then I will peel the rest on the way to Provo and cook when I get there. (3) I hope those are the ones you meant. There is one box left. (4) I took the open mayonnaise jar and left you the new one. (5) I took several plastic bags from the garage box to put peelings [for Velva's cow] and the peeled apples in."[7]

Rose Marie Reid, world famous designer, peeled apples during her drive from Baker, Oregon, to Boise, Idaho, while somebody drove the car. Furthermore, she couldn't resist giving advice to her sister on how to better preserve the apples next year.

Rose Marie peeled all the way from Baker to Boise so the apples wouldn't be wasted. She arrived at Velva's in Boise with a big pot of "brown" apples for Velva to cook. Velva probably didn't know she was coming, and probably didn't want the apples; certainly she didn't want to cook them that early in the morning. But she wouldn't have dared to tell Rose Marie that. (Rose Marie couldn't even waste the peelings, so she fed them to Velva's cow!)

Rose Marie continued to peel more apples all the way to Provo (another eight hours' worth of peeling). Despite her late arrival, she undoubtedly cooked the apples, since, said her daughter Carole, she would not have slept until they were cooked.

In all likelihood, said Carole, her mother probably gave the cooked apples to another family member. "This," said Carole, "is my MOTHER!"

Although some would call Rose Marie's behavior "eccentric," she seemed to have no concept of the millions of dollars that once swirled about her. There was no vestige of selfish pride. She truly felt she had a stewardship over everything entrusted to her care— even apple peelings. She was driven to promote expediency, do what was right, and waste nothing.

"I'm glad I wasn't riding in that car with that sticky mess, said Carole. "Mother wouldn't have even seen it."

On another occasion, Rose Marie was concerned about a couch that needed to be recovered. The matching fabric was simply not available. She immediately knew she had to resolve the problem. The walls were covered with a matching fabric wall covering. The paper backing allowed it to be hung smoothly. She searched the house for leftover rolls of the wall coverings and found some.

Said Carole, "I knew immediately what she was thinking and I pled with her not to do it." Close to delivering her sixth child, Carole went to the hospital, returning to a bathtub full of wallpaper that Rose Marie was soaking to separate the backing from the fabric. Glue and paper were everywhere—all over the floor, walls, and tracked throughout the house. Carole cringed at the sight, but within a few days Rose Marie had sewn the peeled-off fabric pieces together and reupholstered the couch. "Of course," said Carole, "it was beautiful."

Notes

1. Rose Marie Reid, letter to Marion Heilner, 12 June 1966.
2. LeGrand Richards, letter to Rose Marie Reid, 20 April 1971.
3. Rose Marie Reid, letter to Marion Heilner, 11 June 1975.
4. Truman G. Madsen, letter to Rose Marie Reid, 13 June 1963.
5. John A. Widstoe, letter to Rose Marie Reid, 16 May 1952.
6. Rose Marie Reid, Oral History, p. 169.
7. Rose Marie Reid, letter to Marion Heilner, ca. 1969.

CHAPTER 20

"I Will See You Next Easter"

Every morning the little Burr children would cross the driveway and run up the hill to check on their Grandmother Rose Marie, who was usually at her sewing machine making clothes for the family. There they would stop for a fitting before she sent them off to school. Rose Marie loved her grandchildren dearly. The children knew that whatever they couldn't have at home, all they had to do to get it was run to "Grandma's."

Rose Marie read to them, fed them, and became their personal chauffeur. She spent hours walking babies in strollers, guarding them on the trampoline, and pushing the swings. She attended all their church and school programs. The children built forts on her stairway and carved their names in an old table she kept just for them. They dressed up in her clothes, stumbled around in her shoes, and put on her makeup.

"I truly felt," said Carole, "and I often told Mother that she and I had made a very special arrangement during our pre-earth life. We promised each other that I would sacrifice her time with me as a child if she would help me raise my family when I needed her most as an adult. My children and I were so blessed to have her near."

By the late 1960s, it was obvious to all that Rose Marie's health was failing. Her asthma had advanced to the stage that she needed to have daily doses of cortisone, which would often be administered intravenously. A frequent patient at the LDS Hospital in Salt Lake City, Rose Marie said more than once, "I'd be willing to die ten years sooner if I could breathe while I am alive."

Advised to go to the Sunrise Hospital in Las Vegas, Rose Marie spent six weeks in a room that was entirely sterilized. The medical staff carefully introduced every chemical and food into her system in an attempt to determine her sensitivities to those substances that aggravated her lungs and breathing. This proved very successful, and for several years the quality of her life improved considerably.

One morning, the children went as usual to check on their Grandmother Rose Marie. However, they did not stay as they usually did but instead came rushing back home. Carole learned that her children had found Rose Marie sitting in her chair unconscious. The ambulance took her to the hospital, where it was determined that she had suffered a stroke.

Carole found it difficult to watch her mother as Rose Marie's mind and memory retraced the beginning years in the Canadian company. "Mother talked about getting sewing machines in Toronto and hunting for fabrics as her brain was reliving times as a young girl with her family," she said. Fearing she would have another massive stroke, Carole remained at her side at the hospital worried and fatigued.

She recalled the night she heard the sound of a cane accompanied by the distinguished voice of Rose Marie's dear friend, Elder LeGrand Richards. "He was greeting all those he met, and he stopped and entered Mother's room," Carole said. "He looked so fondly at her and then sweetly put his hands on her head and blessed her with the most beautiful prayer I had ever heard. He thanked the Lord for her goodness and greatness and requested that the angels of heaven attend her during this illness." Afterwards, he turned to Carole and said, "Go home and rest, she will be well cared for." At that moment, said Carole, "I truly felt that angels filled her room."

A lifetime of learning was gone in a moment. The stroke greatly inhibited Rose Marie's memory, and she needed months of rehabilitation to help her learn to do again the things she had once done so easily. Now it was an ordeal for Rose Marie to even read a pattern and follow the directions, or to thread her sewing machine.

Her loss of memory was especially aggravating with regard to her knowledge of the scriptures she so loved. A magnificent scriptorian her entire life, Rose Marie could no longer remember the specific references of particular scriptures, although she remembered their content. A popular speaker, she tried to continue her speeches to local groups, but her memory would fail her, so she could no longer accept the invitations that had always been so frequent.

Carole and her family did their best to help Rose Marie through this difficult time. Carole learned to complete Rose Marie's unfinished sentences for her, which alternately gratified and irritated her mother. Carole's children visited their grandmother daily. They sat on her bed and lay beside her—talking for hours, helping her to regain her strength, giving her the will to get well.

In the summer of 1977, Carole and Rose Marie planned a large family reunion for all the descendants of Marie and Elvie Yancey. Rose Marie was thrilled to see her sisters, Marion and Ruth, and her brother Elvie, as well as all their children and grandchildren—over one hundred in all. How great their posterity had become, and how proud her father and mother would be!

The following January, the wife of Elder LeGrand Richards passed away. In response to Rose Marie's letter of condolence, Elder Richards wrote: "I appreciate very much your letter of sympathy in the passing of Sister Richards—she was an angel, and I am sure that is what she is where she is now. Considering my age, I will soon join her there, so I am comforted."[1]

Rose Marie's days were filled with the children and grandchildren she adored, although her nights were filled with pain and the continual struggle for breath. Night after night Carole slept on the floor beside her mother's bed, ready to administer oxygen whenever Rose Marie would awaken, gasping for air.

Rose Marie's beloved sister Marion was at the same time devotedly nursing her husband, Sanford, in their Baker home. Despite her frailness, Rose Marie so greatly wanted to see them that she flew to Baker, but could stay only a few weeks because of her own poor health.

Back in Salt Lake, Rose Marie was again admitted into the hospital, where she underwent surgery. Her extended use of cortisone significantly delayed the healing process, causing a painfully slow recovery. Twice Carole brought her mother home, only to return her once again to the hospital for further treatment.

On 18 November 1978, Heather Lynn Burr, Rose Marie's first great-grandchild, was born while Rose Marie herself was still in the hospital. Some weeks later, on 16 December, Rose Marie was released. Although she was very weak, her improvement was so rapid that within four days she had regained enough strength to visit her dentist. That evening she sat in the family room and folded diapers. Later, her two little granddaughters—Amanda, age two, and Emily, age three—helped feed her dinner in bed, and Susan, who was fourteen, tucked her in for the night. "I love you, Grandma," she said and Rose Marie replied, "I love you, darling." The family then went to a sporting event at the high school two blocks away.

Upon arriving home, twelve-year-old Rose Marie Burr, her granddaughter and namesake, went in to check on Grandmother Rose Marie. A quick glance told her something was amiss, and the young girl returned quickly to her parents. "Mom," she said to Carole, "something is wrong."

Carole climbed the stairs to Rose Marie's room, where she saw her sitting peacefully on her couch. She knelt beside her and touched her, and knew she had gone. "At first I was overcome with grief that she had died alone," said Carole. "A house full of family, and this important experience for her happened all alone. I searched to see if she had struggled for breath, but her face was peaceful. And then I was filled with the knowledge that if I had been there pleading with her to live, it would have been too difficult for her to leave us. She had dedicated her life to us and to others for so long. This way she could return freely to her mother, her brothers—Hugh, Oliver, and Don—into the arms of her beloved father and on to her God."

Looking into her still beautiful face, Carole found herself asking "why I had been so privileged to be her daughter." And though they had struggled many times to save her life, "in death there was no struggle, just a transition into a new state," said Carole. "I personally believe that death is a birth to another life filled with service and the distinct privilege of being with those you love. I knew

Mother would be creating and moving forward, ageless and peaceful, full of purpose. Her measure of creation on this earth was finished, complete.

"She said to me one time, 'I hope that in the spirit world we are not dressed only in white. I would not want to wear only white,' and I knew that somehow she would be adding strands of color to all she beheld, making things lovelier.

"My thoughts went back to our childhood when we would sadly leave Aunt Marion's home in Baker, Oregon. I could hear her saying to me, as she had said so many times to Marion's family, with the same sweet assurance, 'I will see you next Easter, and that will just be the day after tomorrow.'"

Notes

1. LeGrand Richards, letter to Rose Marie Reid, 20 January 1978

Rose Marie Reid is still licensed in many countries of the world today. This design was part of the innovative Rose Marie Reid advertising campaign in the May 1958 California Stylist.

The Name Lives On

In 1990, Sharon was traveling from her home in Denver to Carole's home in Provo. When she returned home two weeks later, she noticed that her jewelry bag was gone. She called Carole and asked: "Please tell me! Did I leave it at your home?" She hadn't, and she was devastated. The jewelry was inherited from Rose Marie—all the most precious things collected during her lifetime in the fashion world and on her world travels. To think that it was gone was too painful to believe. All the memories passed through their minds; every piece had been so important. They were gifts from the past— irreplaceable, wonderful memories.

A year later, while again traveling, Sharon happened to stop at the same motel in Grand Junction, Colorado, as she had the previous year. Throughout the year she had been asking everyone about the jewelry, and now thought to ask the manager of the motel if he knew about the jewelry.

"I have it right here for you," he said. The bag of jewelry was there in his safe. He knew one day the owner would return for it.

As valuable as are the jewels left behind, they are not the most valuable gifts that Rose Marie Reid left for her children. Her true legacy is made up of the intangible beliefs and traditions passed on to her children.

Each of Rose Marie's children received a share of her talent.

Bruce inherited her business genius. Along with the wig company, he created AERCO, a company designed to manufacture a small helicopter for personal use, commissioning two BYU engineers to build a prototype. In another venture he helped pioneer the hydrofoil, a watercraft that lifted itself above the water for faster travel. Creating a company called Checkmate (no connection to the company of the same name today), Bruce also devised a modern bankcard, the forerunner to credit cards like Visa and MasterCharge.

His business partner, Gary Meredith, said "I have never met anyone else in my life as creative as Bruce. He had absolutely more ideas than anyone I have ever seen." Rose Marie was willing "to risk everything for the success of her son," said Dean Chipman.

Rose Marie's daughter Sharon Reid Alden received her sense of design; today she sews out of love and teaches others. She has made hundreds of dresses for young women in her wards and wedding gowns for young brides. She visits her nieces and nephews and upholsters their furniture, making drapes and decorating their homes. Like her mother, she would rather sew and design than do anything else. Recognizing Sharon's talents, Rose Marie emphatically taught her that she could sew for her neighbors, friends and family, but she was to "do it at home, and you stay there with your children."

Carole Reid Burr said, "Mother bequeathed to me a love for all people and a strong desire to share ideas and the revealed truth of the gospel." Using experiences gleaned as a mother of nine children, Carole has written books on parenting, and also sponsors adoptions for childless couples. She has placed over 300 children into loving Mormon homes. "It's a missionary effort, and a wonderful experience to work with these people." Although she rebelliously resisted her mother's lectures about the restored gospel during the long drives between Vancouver and Oregon, Carole now appreciates the gospel. "More than anything," she said, "I love gospel study and teaching."

During her lifetime Rose Marie had received a blessing from her good friend, Truman Madsen, who said to her, "The Lord loves you—not in the ordinary way as we are his children, but specifically he loves you! He knows of the 'secret' ways you have served him as well as the ways you have influenced the whole church."[1]

Charles Norberg, a patriarch in the Church, said of her: "When my hands were on [her] head, I truly realized how greatness and humility can live together. No words have ever flown from my lips with such heavenly rhythm. . . . Heavenly Father framed every phrase, making them like poetry with a heavenly theme. Every promise was great, all the counsel was divine."[2]

Rose Marie's genuine concern and love for others truly set her apart. Five minutes in her presence was all it took to enchant nearly everyone who came in contact with her and felt the beauty of her spirit, as well as her intelligence and grace.

One day, Rose Marie visited with a woman who was self-conscious about her ability to speak English, as it was not her native tongue. Rose Marie encouraged her, saying, "Some people from Holland lived next to us for years, and they did not do as well." And then she added her signature phrase: *"You are a miracle!"*

This phrase, "You are miracle!" was Rose Marie's trademark as a teacher. She used it easily and sincerely, continually seeking to help others feel better about themselves as they worked to develop their potential as children of our Heavenly Father. All people counted in her eyes, and she took valuable time in their care. One woman wrote: "I was hoping you would take the time to suggest a suit for a girl of 24 [with] red loud hair!"[3] Rose Marie answered her personally.

A San Francisco woman wrote: "Thank you very much for taking the time to answer me with your letter of the 19th. I appreciate your suggestions very much. From the description of my figure faults, you seem to be able to pick out the right suit for me, more so than the sales people at the various stores. I will be 44 years of age in July and find myself getting so nervous over every little thing."[4]

In 1989, Rose Marie Burr MacArthur lived in Tsuruga, Japan, where she taught conversational English classes to employees of the Toyoba Company, one of the largest textile companies in the country. She began her first class by introducing herself: "My name is Rose Marie. I am named after my grandmother Rose Marie Reid, who was a designer of swimsuits in the United States."

The class, which held several of the company executives, was suddenly alert. "Rose Marie Reid?!" said one executive, the personnel director. "We provide the fabric for the Rose Marie Reid swimsuits in Japan. We carry the license for her name."

The members of the class were in immediate awe of young Rose Marie. They treated her as if she were a member of royalty, and arranged for her to be introduced to the corporate management, who drove from Osaka to meet her. The CEO of the company even wrote her a personal letter, and young Rose Marie was featured in the company newspaper. She was constantly asked questions about her grandmother's life and was treated with great reverence. "They told me that Rose Marie Reid in Japan was one of the most successful swim suit companies in the country," she said.

Today, Rose Marie Reid is still licensed in many countries of the world and is manufactured in the United States, Japan, Italy, Canada, and England. United Merchants purchased the Jonathan Logan Company, acquiring the licensing rights to the Rose Marie Reid name and manufacturing division in 1986. Based in New York, United Merchants is a diversified company engaged principally in the design and distribution of apparel and accessories as well as the manufacture and distribution of textiles. In 1987, its volume of sales was $14 million, increasing to $15 million in 1990. In 1992, United Merchants sold the Rose Marie Reid division to Sibron Holdings, who design, manufacture, and market swimwear throughout the United States and several other countries.

By 1994 the Sirena Apparel Group, Inc., of Southern California "acquired the trademark, designs, and raw materials relating to Rose Marie Reid. The Sirena Group is one of the largest manufacturers of branded [or brand name] women's swimwear in the United States. Each of the companies' brands (Anne Klein, Look & Sea, WearAbouts, Sirena, and Rose Marie Reid) is among the leaders in its category, and is widely recognized for its fashionable styling, consistent fit, and quality construction."[5]

Twelve years after her mother's death, while Sharon was traveling with her husband, Paul Alden, on a business trip to Europe, she entered Herrod's Department Store in London, where the entire sportswear department featured Rose Marie Reid swimsuits. Delighted to see the success of the Rose Marie Reid line, Sharon said, "How proud I felt that her name was still valued in so many parts of the world and in the United States."

Few women of the 1990s can understand the obstacles that faced a businesswoman in the first half of the twentieth century. With grace and intelligence, Rose Marie overcame the difficulties that confronted her, demonstrating values that are timeless, regardless of the time or the trends: honesty, hard work, respect for one's fellowmen and women—all enhanced by a limitless faith in God.

Throughout her life, Rose Marie's motto consisted of one phrase: "Seek ye first the kingdom of God, and his righteousness; and all these things shall be added unto you" (Matthew 6:33). Her advice to others was simple and unequivocal: Do it the Lord's way. If you are meant to succeed, the Lord will see that it happens. This is a formula for success at any age and for all women. This is the formula embodied by Rose Marie Reid.

Notes

1. Truman G. Madsen, blessing given to Rose Marie Reid, 27 February 1971.
2. Charles H. Norberg, typed letter sent with Rose Marie Reid's patriarchial blessing, July 1951.
3. Unsigned letter to Rose Marie Reid, 12 May 1957 (Kingsville, Texas).
4. Unsigned letter to Rose Marie Reid, 4 April 1958 (San Francisco).
5. Company Prospective, p. 3. This document, which was prepared by Sirena for its stockholders, is in the possession of the authors.

INDEX